# AN
# EMPIRE
## IN RUINS
#### BUT A FORMIDABLE ADVERSARY

# AN
# EMPIRE
## IN RUINS
### BUT A FORMIDABLE ADVERSARY

## ANTWYN PRICE

ARPress
ILLUMINATING IDEAS.
EMPOWERING VOICES

# EAST ASIA WITH F

CHINA

BURMA

LAOS

HAINAN

SOU
CHI
SE.

SIAM

INDOCHINA

CAMBODIA

ANDAMAN
SEA

GULF OF
THAILAND

Britis

Acheh (Atjeh)

MALAYA

Malacca

Sarawak

Singapore

Dutch

SUMATRA

Pladjoe

Pladjoe

DUTCH EAST INDIES

JAVA
SEA

Soenda

Soebang

Batavia (Djakarta)

Tjiater Pass

Soere

Bandoeng

JAVA

Tjilatjap

KOREA JAPAN

MAP AREA

Lourenço
Marques

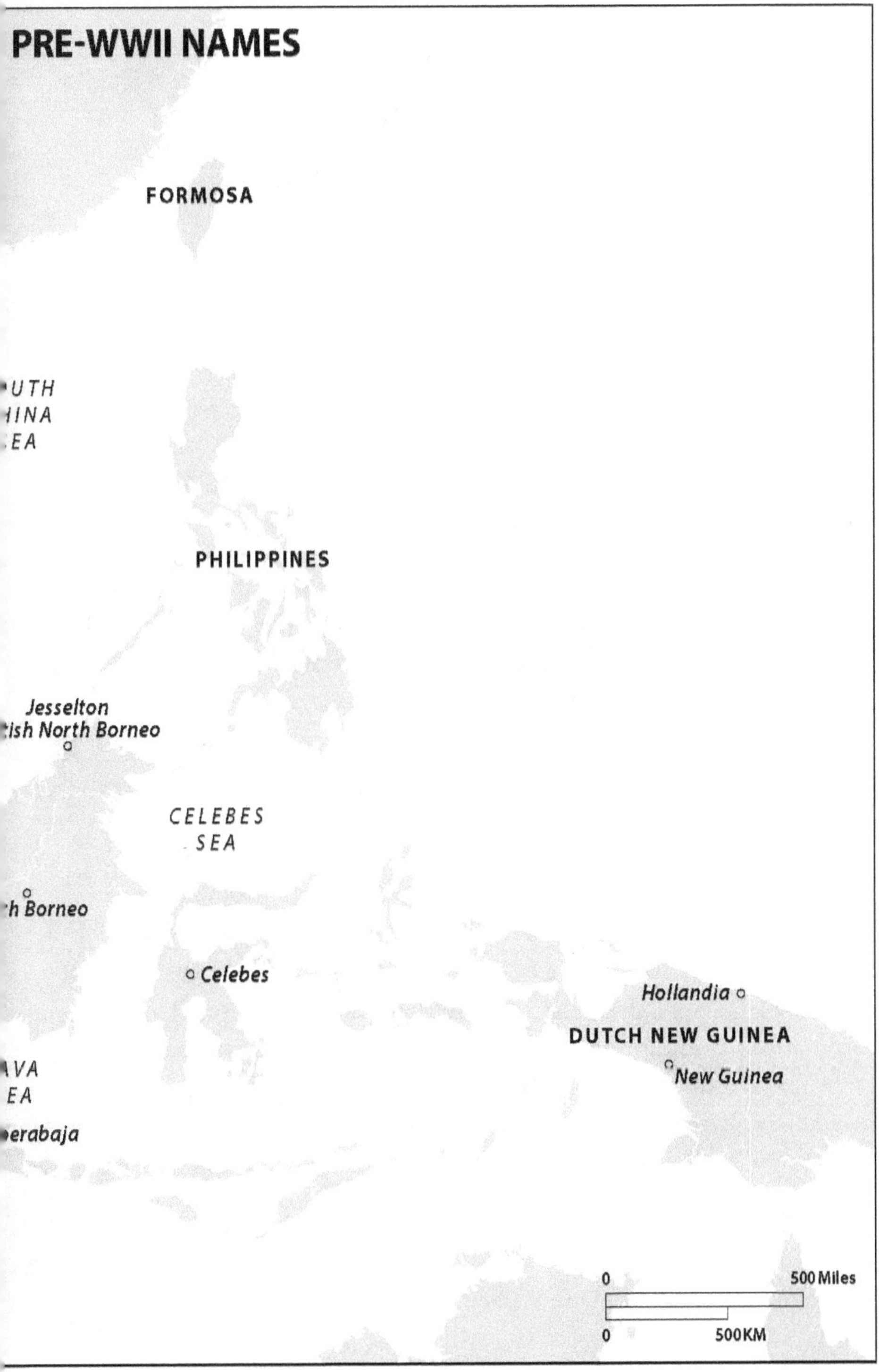

# PRE-WWII NAMES

FORMOSA

*UTH*
*HINA*
*EA*

**PHILIPPINES**

*Jesselton*
*ish North Borneo*
○

*CELEBES*
*SEA*

○
*h Borneo*

○ *Celebes*

*Hollandia* ○

**DUTCH NEW GUINEA**
○ *New Guinea*

*AVA*
*EA*

*erabaja*

| 0 | | 500 Miles |
|---|---|---|
| 0 | | 500 KM |

**ARPress**
45 Dan Road Suite 5
Canton MA 02021
Hotline:           1(888) 821-0229
Fax:               1(508) 545-7580

Ordering Information:

Quantity sales. Special discounts are available on quantity purchases by corporations, associations, and others. For details, contact the publisher at the address above.

Printed in the United States of America.

| ISBN-13: | Softcover | 979-8-89330-287-5 |
|---|---|---|
|  | eBook | 979-8-89330-286-8 |

Library of Congress Control Number: 2024901447

# CONTENTS

# DEDICATIONS

This fictionalized history of World War Two in the Pacific Theater is dedicated to Ms Elizabeth Seligmann Robinson, who also appears from time to time as a character in the story. More often known as Betsy to her friends and family, she was an amazing woman who lived for more than a century, but she never forgot her remarkable adventures in the Pacific with the USO.

This work is also dedicated to Clarence Emil Saegert, who was a Seguin classmate of Betsy's from kindergarten through high school, and who likewise appears as a character in the story. Clarence joined the US Navy Reserve in 1941 and was sent overseas in 1944, leaving behind his pregnant wife Evelyn in Austin, Texas. He did not see their first baby until he returned home from WWII.

## Elizabeth S. Robinson

*Born 9 December 1919 Seguin Texas
*Broadway dancer at age 15
*Stage name Betsy Berkley
*United Service Organization (USO) entertainer during and after WWII
*Fashion buyer and rancher
*Died 5 June 2021 Seguin Texas, age 101
*Buried Fort Sam Houston Cemetery, San Antonio Texas

## Clarence E. Saegert

*Born 10 July 1919 Seguin Texas
*Attended Texas Lutheran College in Seguin
*BS with honors U. Texas, Austin
*WWII PT-Boat Skipper (PT-105)
*Postwar career in PR and advertising
*Austin Chamber of Commerce
*Austin Symphony board
*Died 25 Feb 1980 Austin Texas, age 60
*Buried Oakwood Cemetery, Austin

# Epigraphs

*Thirty-seven USO entertainers died during World War II. The most famous one who did not make it back was legendary big band leader and then-Army Major Glenn Miller, whose plane disappeared over the English Channel on the way to France in December 1944.*

USO website


*They were made of wood, carried no heavy guns, and would sink at the drop of a hat. But they were fast, hard to hit, and could kill nearly anything afloat. Pound for pound, the deadliest boats of World War II weren't the carriers or the legendary battleships, they were the humble patrol torpedo boats.*

We Are\*The Mighty website

# INTRODUCTION

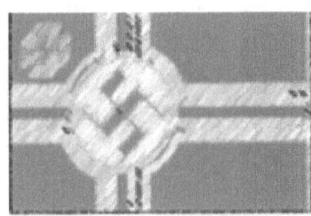

*Stylized Flags of Germany, Italy, and Japan in WWII*

This slightly fictionalized history, **An Empire in Ruins** (2022), is the author's third book of a trilogy about WWII in the Pacific. The others are **Paradise in Ruins** (2019) and **Colonies in Ruins** (2020). The three books are aimed at recreating a world for their readers that began fading away nearly eighty years ago after the most disruptive and wasteful cataclysm in human history, the Second World War.

While the first two books dealt with rear-echelon events during the Pacific war (**Paradise**), and the loss of American and European possessions in the Pacific region as a result of the war (**Colonies**), this final book of the series (**Empire**) provides an overview of the major Pacific war battles and a look at the postwar occupation of Japan.

Including many interesting photos of the era, **An Empire in Ruins** focuses on the combatants from both sides of the conflicts—their fears and anxieties, their courage under fire, and their willingness to die for a cause. We could all ask ourselves about those same attributes, no doubt, but it is sometimes safer to assess these qualities in others.

There is a lot to absorb for readers who are not familiar with WWII, so we suggest taking things slowly and digesting a chapter at a time. The Second World War provides a huge canvass for study. Many authors have written about the conflict from different perspectives, and some titles may be found in our bibliography for recommended further reading.

**An Empire in Ruins** uses both fictional and real characters to convey the drama and emotions of this very important period of history that transformed our world. Since it may not be obvious which people in the story are historical and which are fictional, please refer to the End Notes for a list of the fictional ones. Should any of those resemble actual persons, living or dead, it is accidental and unintentional.

**Verisimilitude**—All other named characters are historical, to whom various words or actions have been attributed by the author with the utmost respect, to enhance and enliven their known public personae.

**Orthography**—US spelling is used in this historical novel, with apologies in advance to our British readers!

**Our Readers**—Very few veterans of WWII are still alive today, but some readers may have parents or grandparents who were involved in the dark days of 1941-45 or the transformative postwar decade that led to the world in which we now live. World War Two veterans typically did not talk much about their wartime experiences. This book should help explain why that was so.

**This Trilogy:** World War Two left almost every Pacific Island *Paradise in Ruins*. After the war, the region's *Colonies in Ruins* were transformed into new nations. A series of horrendous battles left *An Empire in Ruins* that had intended to conquer the Pacific region.

If the books of this trilogy were an interesting read for you, perhaps you will be kind enough to leave some comments on your bookstore's website for others to see. Thank you!

# PROLOGUE

## *** THE WAR IN EUROPE ***

Far too soon after the devastations of World War One, a new war in Europe began with a lightning strike—Blitzkrieg—by German forces into Poland on September 1st, 1939, without a formal declaration of war. Claiming to be retaliation for a Polish incursion into Germany the previous day, which had been stage-managed by the Germans themselves, Nazi Germany's leader Adolf Hitler lied to the world that he had no alternative but to retaliate.

In short order, Germany attacked by land, sea, and air to quickly subjugate Poland's obsolete army. This in turn encouraged Soviet Russia (although not a German ally) to invade Poland a few weeks later, after which the devastated country was partitioned between the two invaders. Even after Germany's Nazi forces tried to conquer Russia itself—but were repelled in 1945 at the Battle of Stalingrad—Poland remained under the thumb of Russia until the collapse of the Soviet Union in 1989.

How did this new disaster come about for Poland, and how did Germany, having been defeated and economically ruined by the First World War, obtain the wherewithal to design and manufacture enough modern weaponry to defeat such a large neighboring country as Poland, and then go on to subjugate much of western Europe? Please read on to find out.

## *** HITLER'S RISE TO POWER ***

In 1918, after Germany's defeat in the Great War (WWI), a workers' party called DAP was formed, which army-veteran Adolf Hitler was invited to join because of his exceptional oratory skills and suitably anti-liberal outlook. DAP later became the National Socialist, or Nazi Party which was ultra-nationalistic, anti-Semitic, anti-capitalist, and anti-Marxist. In 1920, Hitler spoke to a crowd of 2,000 at the Munich Hofbrauhaus, outlining DAP's foreign policy wishes which were (1) to abrogate the Treaty of Versailles, (2) to prevent Jews from holding citizenship, and (3) to create a powerful Germany to dominate its neighbors.

Hitler attracted malcontented people like bees to pollen with his strident anti-everything oratories, knowing the majority of Germans hated their own Weimar Republic's liberal government and the Treaty of Versailles whereby the victorious Allies were exacting punishing

*Adolf Hitler*

retributions from Germany for having started the Great War that destroyed untold property and lives in other countries, notably France.

Hitler promised his many followers to restore Germany's imagined greatness, with a sort of "Make Germany Great Again" manifesto.

The Versailles peace treaty also forced Germany to give up certain adjacent territories to France, Poland, and Denmark, which caused intense resentment among the German populace. Meanwhile, after the Bolshevik Revolution in Russia and the brutal murder of the Czar and his family, Marxism was on the lookout for unstable countries all over the world on which to prey or proselytize. Among several other nations, such as China (which succeeded) and Mexico (which failed), Germany with its post-war gloom was a prime target.

Thus the neophyte German Communist Party gave Hitler yet another group—together with the Jews and the "bloodsucking capitalists"—on which to focus the collective anger of his followers who, he would shout, were being forced to take the blame for Germany's current sorry condition instead of "the despicable Jews who had actually betrayed it" (a fomented rumor that had been in circulation ever since Germany's defeat).

Nazi membership swelled even further after the 1929 market crash in the US, which affected many other countries including Germany. This "Worldwide Great Depression" during the early 1930s resulted in millions being out of work in Germany and elsewhere.

After Hitler was appointed Chancellor (Head of Government) in 1933, in a failed attempt by President von Hindenburg (Head of State at the Reichstag) to appease him through power sharing, there was soon an end to any trace of German democracy. Hitler consolidated his power over the army, the police, and the civil service, and banned all other political parties. Germany thus became a police state in short order.

*Deutschland, Deutschland über Alles*— "Germany Over All" (meaning above everyone else) had become the new National Anthem as the country gradually got back on its feet after the previous war that it had lost. *[That uplifting tune by Franz Haydn is still the German National Anthem today, but with the original first and second militant verses deleted –Ed.].*

In 1933, Hitler announced to its international creditors that Germany would no longer pay WWI reparations that were bankrupting the country and causing hyperinflation. This bold but illegal moratorium, which lasted until the end of WWII in 1945, was what allowed Germany to secretly re-arm. *[The final renegotiated German reparations for both WWI and WWII were not paid off until 2010. Banker über Alles!–Ed.].*

Hitler rapidly issued decrees that centralized his control over all Germany, by replacing state governors with Nazi Party members such as Hermann Goering in Prussia, a powerful state. His police and street-fighting volunteer brown-shirt SA "storm troopers" rained terror upon trade unions, corporations, religious organizations, and any individuals that sought to resist his power.

Soon a Nazi private army emerged, having originally been a small militia to provide security for Hitler and senior party members. They were the black-shirted SS under Heinrich Himmler that pushed aside the SA. Himmler also created a plain-clothed secret police—the *Gestapo*—from within the regular police organization, to further terrorize and arrest those who refused to obey Nazi laws and policies.

During 1933, the Dachau concentration camp was established by Himmler in a disused munitions building from the first war. Here the Gestapo and SS began to lock up and torture enemies of the state such as Trade Unionists, Communists, and Socialists. Before long, Germany would be operating many more such concentration camps.

Not long after Dachau was opened, a roundup of Jews took place. The unlucky victims were taken to various concentration camps as the Nazi "final solution" began, the extermination of Jews by murder and incineration. This mass-killing spree would later become known as The Holocaust. Although a quarter of the terrified German Jewish population had left Germany by this time, most of the remainder would find it impossible to obtain visas even from Britain and the USA which had both condemned Germany's treatment of the Jews.

Eventually some six million entrapped Jews lost their lives in Germany and within the countries that Germany overran during WWII.

# *** THE SPANISH CIVIL WAR ***

During 1936-39, in what was later regarded as a preamble to the Second World War, Spanish Nationalists (Conservatives and Catholics) fought to unseat Spain's Republican (Liberal and Anti-Monarchist) government. After nearly three years of bitter fighting, the Nationalists prevailed with the aid of troops and materials from Italy and Germany. Germany provided some 600 planes and 200 tanks and benefitted from the live training that the Spanish conflict provided to Luftwaffe pilots. There were even German volunteers that formed the "Condor Unit" to fight on the side of the Nationalists. When the Nationalists won and the Republican government was toppled, General Francisco Franco assumed the Spanish presidency and ruled as a dictator for many decades until his death in 1975. It is estimated that a million people were killed in this brutal and fiercely contested civil war.

## *** ENGLAND'S FINEST HOURS ***

After Germany (and the Soviet Union) invaded Poland, war quickly spread to the rest of Western Europe. Before long, Poland, Czechoslovakia, Denmark, Norway, Belgium, Holland, and France had all fallen to German advances. France was then partitioned into two zones—a pro-German zone under former Marshall Philippe Petain, administered in the city of Vichy; and an occupied zone administrated by Germany itself. Later a small portion of the Vichy zone was placed under the control of Mussolini's Italy, which had the task of ensuring that the rest of Vichy stayed loyal to the German-Italian Axis.

There was also a nascent Free French government in exile under General Charles de Gaulle that was sheltered in London, as was the Dutch government in exile.

Some French overseas colonies in the Pacific region, like Indochina, allied themselves with the Vichy government and were thereby safe havens for Germans (and later on for Japanese), but others such as New Caledonia supported the Free French and were used by the Allies early on as bases against German commerce-raiding warships in the Pacific, and eventually against Japan after it joined the Axis war effort.

After the fall of France in 1940, Great Britain—the kingdom of England, Scotland, Ireland, and Wales—suddenly found itself fighting alone against the Axis of Germany and Italy in Continental Europe and North Africa. Thousands of British troops stationed in France were miraculously evacuated at Dunkirk on the English Channel by British

Royal Navy ships and scores of small civilian-owned boats, and thereby saved from German concentration camps. Dunkirk was a demeaning but successful retreat.

Soon afterwards, Great Britain—especially London its capital—was heavily raided on a daily and nightly basis by German bombers, an ordeal that lasted for several grim months. Against those constant bombing raids, a relatively small cohort of Spitfire and Hurricane fighter planes flown by young British and expatriate Polish pilots managed to repeatedly cull the overwhelming superiority of German bombers, and in the end, with the help of newly invented radar, they prevailed—amid great jubilation—to see Germany cancel its invasion plans.

*Sir Winston Churchill*

Britain's prime minister Winston Churchill made a series of stirring speeches to the House of Commons during those desperate months, many of which are still quoted today as a tribute to his unique oratory skills. *(If only the forthcoming world war could have been confined to a public debate between Churchill and Hitler! –Ed.)*

## *** A NEW POTENTIAL FOE ***

The US intelligence services had been keeping a wary eye on Japan ever since that island nation joined the Tripartite Pact with Germany and Italy in September 1940. Draft conscription was started in the US that same month, requiring all men between the ages of 18 and 45 to register, which no doubt jolted a portion of the "pro-neutrality" population. *[That 1940 draft law was not repealed until 1973, after having also supported both the Korean and Vietnam conflicts—Ed.]*

Soon after 1937 when Japan invaded China, the US sent the 4th Marine Regiment to guard the International Settlement in Shanghai, even though that part of Shanghai was theoretically a neutral territory. The 4th Marines made themselves quite visible in order to keep international residents from panicking as news of Japanese atrocities in other parts of China became widely known.

*4th Marines on parade in Shanghai*

When Japanese troops were allowed into southern Indochina in July 1941, having already captured Manchuria and much of coastal China, US intelligence efforts were intensified with the realization that Japan had made that latest aggressive move in order to block China's only remaining access to the Pacific Ocean, and also to gain access to Indochina's deep-water harbors such as Cam Ranh Bay. Because French Indochina had aligned itself with Vichy France; Japanese troop movements went through it unopposed, although unpopular.

Shortly afterwards, in response, the United States issued an embargo against Japan that effectively curtailed her supplies of oil and steel. In spite of this provocative US action and its enhanced scrutiny of Japan's militancy in Asia, warnings for a Japanese retaliatory attack on Pearl Harbor in Hawaii somehow "fell through the cracks," as the expression goes.

Sanctions on Japan were later seen as a tragic blunder on the part of US leadership, but were they? Pearl Harbor was sheltering a nearly obsolete fleet of battleships while a crucial trio of aircraft carriers was elsewhere on maneuvers, thereby escaping Japan's fearsome attack. It was those carriers that would lead the US counterattacks against Japan just a few months later in the battles of the Coral Sea and Midway. Above all, the Pearl Harbor attack instantly shook America out of its remaining neutrality stance and enabled US troops to be sent to Britain in preparation for a steady buildup that would lead the charge across the English Channel a year later.

# *** SUPPORT FOR BRITAIN AND RUSSIA ***

In spite of the alarming war news from Europe as Great Britain struggled alone against the growing Axis of Nazi Germany and Fascist Italy, most Americans at home firmly insisted on neutrality *(and some were even supportive of Hitler and Mussolini – Ed.)*. US President Franklin Delano Roosevelt (known by the Press Corps as FDR) was torn between a need to support the American people's wishes by remaining neutral, and his instinctive desire to help Britain during its time of great need. His eventual solution became known as Lend Lease, an arrangement whereby the US would—in theory—lease ships and planes to the British, but which was in reality a donation.

When the US and Germany declared war on each other in December 1941, soon after Japan's attack on Pearl Harbor, Roosevelt's sense of responsibility resulted in massive convoys of ships sailing from US ports, escorted by American destroyers on the lookout for German submarines (which were called Undersea Boats or U-Boats) that hunted in lethal "wolf packs" in an effort to destroy the convoys. The U-Boats refueled in neutral places like Iceland and Portugal, and occasionally from their own undersea tankers, at first beginning their deadly attacks within sight of the American coastline. During the deadly game of torpedoes-versus-depth charges within the Atlantic crossings, hundreds of US warplanes were also being ferried by air to Britain's RAF—many flown by women pilots—at risk of being shot down by Hitler's *Luftwaffe* as they approached the British Isles.

After 1941 waned toward 1942, American ocean convoys gradually prevailed over German U-Boats and the air convoys likewise prevailed. US production ramped up to support Britain's war against Germany—and also to help Russia, which was fiercely defending itself against a massive German land and air attack that had taken place in June 1941 as a gambit by Hitler to destroy Communism. Without this abrupt flood of orders for modernized military and naval resources, the United States might not have been able to retaliate against the other terrific blow that was to come from a different quarter—Japan!

On the other hand, supplying Britain and Russia with military aid did create shortages for the US Marine Corps that was expected to blunt Japanese aggression in the Pacific with World War One light tanks and bolt-action rifles. They managed to do so anyway at Guadalcanal, but the US loss of life would have been much less with the M4 medium tanks and semi-automatic M1 rifles that came along later when the US Army arrived in the Pacific.

As tensions grew in the Pacific even before the Pearl Harbor disaster, it was finally decided to move the 4th Marine Regiment out of Shanghai, since many international banks and other businesses there had already begun moving their personnel away. The 4th Marines were instead sent to Manila to beef up the US naval base at Cavite and the coastal defenses of Manila Bay while General MacArthur commenced a belated training regimen for the Philippine Army.

Meanwhile, one hundred American volunteer pilots known as the Flying Tigers were formed into three squadrons by retired USAAF Major General Claire Chennault to help Nationalist China defend the Burma Road, which was a crucial inland supply route. The flyers were former Army, Navy and Marine pilots who had been discharged from their services so that they could be hired as paid civilian volunteers. They flew Curtis P40 aircraft that were painted with distinctive shark tooth cowlings, and were credited with the destruction of nearly 300 Japanese planes before being disbanded a few months after the US officially joined the war in the Pacific. Thirty-three of the brave volunteer pilots were lost in combat with Japan.

*(The author had the pleasure of dining often in the 1980s at the former Shanghai home of Gen. Chennault and his wife Anna Chen, which had been converted into a small but charming restaurant – Ed.)*

*Chinese soldier guarding Flying Tiger aircraft in Kunming, China*

# CHAPTER ONE

## *** WAR IN THE PACIFIC ***

*USS West Virginia on fire at Pearl Harbor 7 December 1941*

## *** THE PEARL HARBOR ATTACK ***

Japan and China had been actively at war since 1937, but there was little public interest in that far-away conflict by a US public that was chiefly concerned about what was happening in Europe, where many Americans had ancestral ties. This was true even though Japan had managed to take control of China's coastal provinces and had committed massive atrocities in Chinese cities such as Nanking. It was the war in Europe that sold American newspapers.

But when the Empire of Japan abruptly attacked the United States of America's naval base in Hawaii in a similar unannounced way to Germany's sudden and undeclared invasions of Poland and Russia, it was a wake-up call for the US Congress which had been steadfast in its support of neutrality up to that point. Suddenly everything was changed and "the gloves were off." Within a day, Congress declared war on Japan. Then Germany and Italy declared war on the United States as the Tripartite Pact obliged them to do; the US reciprocated promptly.

The massive Pearl Harbor attack was a great tactical success for Japan. Soon after daylight on Sunday 7 December 1941, successive waves of warplanes from six Japanese aircraft carriers that had been secretly underway from Japan for two weeks, struck the Naval Base at Pearl Harbor, Territory of Hawaii, intent on sinking the US Pacific

Fleet's battleships moored in pairs around Ford Island. This well planned attack, conceived by Harvard-educated and highly decorated Japanese Admiral Yamamoto, sent the battleships *Arizona* and *Oklahoma* permanently to the bottom and damaged six more battleships, three cruisers, and three destroyers *(that were eventually put back into service —Ed.)*. With significant loss of life at the naval air station, US Army and Marine planes and ground facilities were also destroyed by Japanese fighter planes that swooped back and forth as they

Fleet Admiral Yamamoto Isoroku (山本 五十六)

strafed the awakening facility, then returned to their offshore carriers to refuel and attack again. Choosing an early Sunday morning for the attack was a shrewd choice by Admiral Yamamoto, knowing from Japanese spies in Hawaii that most military and naval personnel would be sleeping off Saturday night hangovers and US resistance would be light. Equally shrewd was taking the fleet on past Hawaii to attack it from the east, knowing American planes would search for it to the west. In fact, radar at Pearl Harbor did detect the Japanese planes en route from the east, but no alarm was raised as it was assumed to be an expected inbound flight of US planes from California.

*Japanese photo of the initial bombing raid on Ford Island in Pearl Harbor*

## *** THE OFFICE OF NAVAL INTELLIGENCE **

Shortly before the surprise attack, newly promoted, collegiate-looking Navy Lieutenant Commander Elmer "Bongo" Perkins was among those unfortunates who were assigned to the skeleton Sunday morning duty roster at various naval facilities on Oahu and a few other Hawaiian Islands. His plain-clothes assignment was Duty Officer at a semi-secret ONI (Office of Naval Intelligence) facility near downtown Honolulu, the Hawaiian capital. The little house that had been acquired by the ONI for interrogations and the occasional boozy party was nondescript looking outside but had the latest radio and telephone equipment stowed in a back room.

Bongo—a name that he had earned from friends by drumming occasionally with a dance band at the Moana Hotel—was slightly irritated at having to stand a security watch that would normally be assigned to ensigns or junior lieutenants. On the other hand, he knew there was only one such junior officer in this particular clandestine Naval Intelligence organization, and that young fellow had just retired after standing the previous midnight's "graveyard shift."

*Oh joy,* Bongo says to himself as he pours yet another cup of bitter Navy coffee. He scarcely adds his customary two spoonsful of sugar before hearing muffled explosions coming from distant Pearl Harbor. Then comes heavy gunfire and multiple aircraft engines roaring far away and a few more closely.

*Uh-oh; what the hell was that?* he mumbles as he drops the hot cup into the small kitchen sink. *Looks like something big!* he realizes as a wailing ambulance speeds past the shuttered front windows.

"Hey McGowan, wake the hell up!" Bongo bangs and shouts through the doorway of another little back room with a pair of over-and-under bunks that he and the presently-snoring Ensign Robert McGowan use whenever they have the weekend duty. "Quickly, man, get a hold of yourself ... now!"

"Mmm...OK sir, be right there,' the young ensign manages to say as he struggles to pull on his civilian trousers and flowered Aloha shirt, and hurries to the head for a quick pee. "What's up...er, sir?"

"Hell, I don't exactly know yet, but there's a lot of unauthorized noise out there." Bongo paces about impatiently until McGowan reemerges. "It sounds like huge explosions and firing over at Pearl, except there are planes flying around outside of here as well, and I can hear the Coastguard shooting at something—maybe those planes. Let's grab some hardware and go find out!"

"Right away, sir," McGowan replied, "But we don't want people to see us with the heavy stuff, right?"

"That's right, of course that's right. Just get us a couple of .45s and let's take a look-see."

Bongo hurriedly leads the way to the nearby harbor boulevard after the pair strap holstered pistols beneath their Hawaiian shirts. Across that thoroughfare they can clearly see USCGC *Taney's* guns blazing away from the Pier 6 Coast Guard dock a mere two hundred yards away near the Aloha Tower, at a trio of roaring fighter planes that seem to be making for the Honolulu power plant. One of the planes is hit, and as it falls toward the harbor the two Navy officers can see large red circles on the wings. They can also hear some faint cheers coming from the Coast Guard cutter.

"Look, they're Jap planes, McGowan!" shouts Bongo over the noise. "Run back and call Cap'n Whatzisname at the Navy Base! Tell him what's going on over here and find out what the heck is happening at Pearl, OK?. I'm going aboard *Taney* to check in with the big boss and see what our orders are."

"Aye, aye sir," McGowan responds very excitedly, suppressing an automatic salute before running back into the safe house. Bongo hurries across the shoreside boulevard and along Pier 6 to where the *Taney* is tied up and still shooting from time to time.

Stopping to catch his breath next to *Taney*'s gangplank, Bongo shouts and waves his ID card at the OD up on deck, "Get the skipper for me, fast! Tell him Commander Perkins would like a word!"

"Aye, aye sir!" The Officer of the Deck heads for the *Taney*'s bridge. Bongo is normally more cautious about pulling his Navy rank while in civilian clothes, but this is an emergency, and he is already acquainted with *Taney* and many of her crew from earlier adventures.

The OD returns: "Please come aboard sir and follow me. The skipper will meet you in the wardroom."

Bongo nods and quickly climbs the ladder as the OD unlocks the upper gate, then he pauses to salute the US flag at the stern. Together they reach the wardroom in a few hurried steps to find Commander Louis B. Olson entering from the other side. He gestures at Bongo to be seated and dismisses the OD with a polite nod

"So what have we got here, Lou?" Bongo begins, as another machine gun burst from Taney's twin 50-calliber turret cuts off their conversation. Bongo and the Coastguard skipper were classmates at the University of Colorado a decade before, hence the familiarity, but Olson was commissioned in the Coast Guard two years before Perkins received his Navy commission after deciding to take master's degree in oriental languages at Dartmouth University.

"Well, this is certainly not a drill, and that's official. We're hearing it's a huge Jap raid on Pearl," says the skipper. They told us to hang in here and guard the city, and sure enough some planes just tried to strafe the power plant. We got one of them and the other two skittered away. But how can we help you, Bongo?"

"Can I use your gear to radio my boss's boss, Admiral Brady? He's been on Maui with some VIPs, and our shore radios can't connect with their PT-Boat...which is a problem I've been trying to fix for-ever, especially since this admiral is also the boss of the PT Boats."

"Sure thing, though there's a hell of a lot of traffic on the air right now. But let's give it a whirl. Come on up to the bridge. What's the boat's call sign that he's on?"

"Heck, I dunno; but the boat is PT-3 from MTB RON-1. Funny thing, by the way," Bongo adds as they hurry up to the bridge, "Admiral Brady's first name is Ronald, or Ron for short. He thinks the RON-designation for his MTB-PT squadron is named after him, when it's really the last three letters of the word Squad-RON!"

"Well, we'll have to drink to that one day, Bongo. But what exactly does MTB mean?"

"Motor Torpedo Boat. It's the British terminology for this kind of boat design, which we basically copied after buying a few of them from the Brits ... or swapping them for Lend-Lease maybe. Once we started building these fighting boats ourselves at Elco and Higgins, the Navy decided to use MTB numbers for squadron IDs and PT numbers for the boats themselves. Good plan, eh? Ah, here we are. Is that your radio shack?" Bongo asks, pointing to an alcove to the rear of the bridge.

"Off limits to anyone but me and the operators, I'm afraid," the *Taney* skipper replies, "but they will try to raise your PT-3 and let us know if they can. Meanwhile, have a look around the harbor if you like. Seems the shooting is over now ... Oh, OK, here we go ... Right, you are patched to that phone over there, Bongo, go ahead and talk."

Nodding his thanks, Bongo takes the offered handset. "Lieutenant Commander Perkins here, over. Is this Admiral Brady?.... Um, yessir.... .yessir..... yessir... mmm... yessir.... Aye, aye sir.... damn... yessir... Roger that. Over and out!"

"Whew, we are in deep sneakers." Bongo takes Commander Olson aside and speaks in a low voice. "Lou, the Jap raid was devastating. Admiral Ron got an update from Lt. Caldwell on his PT command boat at Pearl. Most of the battleships are damaged or sunk, can you believe? Some cruisers and destroyers as well. The airfield is a mess with many of our planes destroyed on the ground and probably plenty of people dead or wounded—they don't know the casualties yet. Anyway, the other PTs 4 through 9 apparently splashed some of the Jap planes with their 50-cal turrets—at least that's something—but it looks like our Pacific Fleet is out of business. Unbelievable! But at least they didn't get the carriers, which are away."

"Well, *Taney* has to stay here and wait for Coast Guard—or maybe Navy—orders," the skipper tells Bongo. "So what are your orders?"

"Can't tell you that, sorry Lou, but I need to get back ashore. It's been a hell of a morning so far."

Bongo's Navy orders are to get hold of the Shore Patrol and have them round up all Japanese-Americans in Hawaii and lock them up somehow. As he hurries back from the Coast Guard cutter toward the ONI safe house to change into his uniform, he ponders these orders. *How the heck can the Shore Patrol alone possibly accomplish this task? Even with Army help, it would be damn near impossible. Where in the world could we lock up over a third of the population? And how in the heck did I end up with this assignment, just because my immediate boss Commodore*

*Stanley "Stoney" Wall is on leave in the States, lucky fellow. Oh well, let's try to get started.*

## *** JAPANESE WAR FLEETS ***

As the six Japanese aircraft carriers and their powerful escorts of the Mobile Force (*Kido Butai*) of the Combined Fleet leave their position two hundred miles northeast of Oahu, and sail back westward toward Japan, several other heavily armed Japanese fleets are already at sea with the intention of invading neutral Thailand (formerly known as Siam) and all British and American colonies that are close to Japan.

Thailand's understrength garrison falls to the Japanese in a matter of hours after being invaded by land from Indochina in the north and by sea at the Kra Isthmus in the south. A week later the king and government promptly agree to become a Japanese ally! Learning that Japanese troops in Thailand are a mere fifty miles north of Malaya—and perhaps even inside Malaya itself at Kota Bharu—greatly alarms the British in Singapore, many of whose Australian and Indian troops are quite busy fighting German General Rommel's tanks in North Africa and thus unavailable to respond aggressively to the Japanese threat.

In addition to Thailand and Malaya, additional Japanese targets for their war fleets, which are preceded by strategic air attacks, include British Hong Kong, Borneo, and Singapore; the Philippines and other US colonies including Wake Island and Guam; and eventually Dutch Java, Sumatra, Borneo, and the Spice Islands known as Maluku. Being across the International Dateline from Hawaii, the British and American colonies receive their attacks on December 8th—some lasting a few days and others several weeks or months for the Japanese before a successful conclusion.

Some Japanese fleets originate in the ample harbors of French Indochina, which Japan had occupied in late 1940 in order to cut off China's only remaining access to the sea. Japan's overall intent is to create an impregnable arc of militarized islands in the mid-Pacific to keep the US and its allies away from their homeland, and above all to protect the crucial oil supplies in the Dutch East Indies once they are under Japan's control.

Even before the United States of America had issued sanctions against Japan by cutting off oil and steel supplies in an attempt to force Japan to stop its hostilities in China, capturing the Dutch oil wells was a foremost objective of Emperor Hirohito, Japan's hereditary ruler. The US sanctions had simply established a date for the various Japanese attacks.

Many people in the United Staes later blame Roosevelt's sanctions for having started the Pacific war but don't realize that Japan had been preparing for war with America and Britain for some years, using China as a training ground (an idea that nudged Hitler to use the Spanish civil war for Germany's training).

## *** ABOARD THE JAPANESE TROOPSHIPS ***

Silent and tense, the thousands of Japanese soldiers who are soon to land in barges at several foreign destinations, pray silently to their ancestors and for their emperor as their troopships plod along at 10 knots, with individual convoys under escort by destroyers on the lookout for American submarines. Almost half of the soldiers are veterans of fighting in China who know the adrenaline rush that comes from facing an enemy when their own life hangs in the balance. Many have gladly killed Chinese "bandits," which is what their leaders call anyone who opposes them, and some of the veterans have been wounded in China and returned to fight again.

Down in the hold below the lower deck—the worst location of all in the old *Maru*-type cargo ships—the rest are downcast young recruits still in their boyhood, who hold the veterans in awe and are afraid to speak to them. They sit apart out of fear and respect, and only glance up when their ship lurches as a rogue wave tosses them about, or when one of the veterans in charge of them stands to urinate through the wooden slats that cover the bilge, or asks a comrade for a cigarette. Overlaying the thump-thump of propellor shafts, the odor of urine and cigarette smoke grows more and more sickening and powerful as the hours wear on, especially for the lengthier convoys from Formosa to the Philippines.

Quite often a young soldier would vomit in the bilge from seasickness, which adds to the foul-smelling atmosphere. An occasional veteran sharpens his already well-honed bayonet while glaring through the smoky haze at the raw recruits across the cargo hold in which they all fester, as if to say that there is far worse to come.

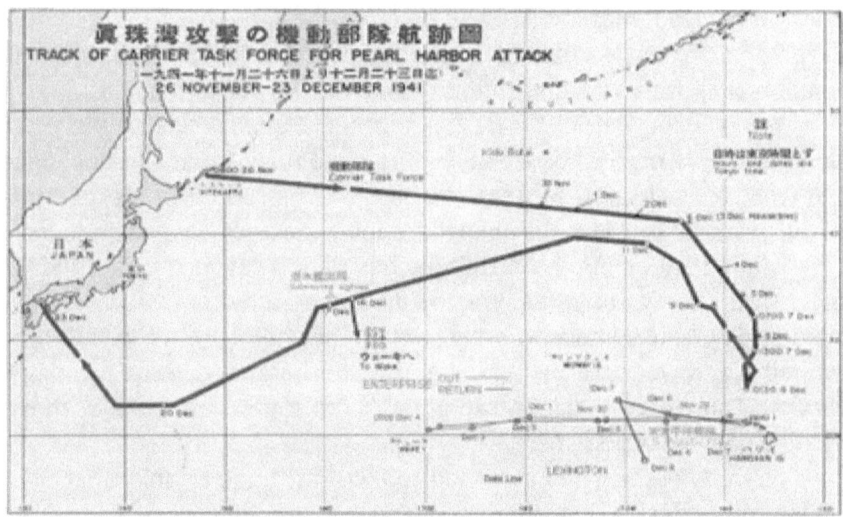

*Route of Japan's Kido Butai Carrier Fleet in December 1941*

By contrast, jubilation reigns within the victorious *Kido Butai* ships that are speeding home from the huge raid in the Hawaiian Islands, in spite of the loss of some veteran pilots and crew members. The Mobile Force flagship for Admiral Nagumo Chûichi is the large new aircraft carrier *Akagi*, whose support fleet includes two battleships, several cruisers and many destroyers that diligently protect all six aircraft carriers. The powerful Japanese fleet, having only lost a few midget submarines in the attack on Hawaii, sets a homeward course that is far away from any islands, even uninhabited ones. Admiral Nagumo knows that all the world will be searching for them, and he does not wish any prying eyes to report his location and fleet composition. It will take fifteen days for the flotilla to reach home by its mid-Pacific route, even at high speed, whereas it had taken twelve days to reach Hawaii by the northern route for the glorious victory—nearly a month of total transit and refueling for the few hours of battle. *The Emperor and Admiral Yamamoto will certainly be pleased by the* Kido Butai *actions, and rightly so*, thinks Admiral Nagumo as he enters the cabin to remove his ceremonial sword.

### ***PANIC AT HOME ***

When news about Pearl Harbor hits the papers and radio broadcasts late on December 7th, panic, consternation, and anger sweep the United States mainland in successive waves of emotion.

"Oh my God, Momma! They'll be bombing here next," shouts Betsy Seligmann, anxiously awaiting her mother, who has just opened the door to enter their New York apartment. "What are we going to do?"

"You're right, darling," says her mother, Blanche, closing the door behind her. "All my friends are saying the same thing—that we should get out while it's still safe!" Mother and daughter hug and tremble together in the entranceway, Blanche almost dropping the door key and her purse.

"Momma, let's book the train or bus right away, or I could find us a car to drive back to Texas. We could be packed by tomorrow—no, by Wednesday, 'cause I have to bring some things home from the club that are mine. But we could be packed and out of here in the next two days, though. Can we do that? Oh Momma, I'm so frightened. Look at those terrible photos in the paper!"

"Hush, sweetheart. I'm worried too, but let's don't panic. That only makes for confusion. Let's have some supper and then sit down to plan things carefully. We don't want to make any mistakes, right?"

Petite and dark-haired Betsy Seligmann from Seguin Texas is twenty-two when the Pearl Harbor attack takes place. She is around five feet eight inches in height, quite trim and athletic looking, and has been dancing in dozens of shows for the past seven years while her divorced mother comes to stay with her in New York off and on as a companion and chaperone. Betsy is known to some New York fans as the "Texas Showgirl" or simply "Tex," while others know her as Betsy Berkley, her official stage name that is sometimes included in very small print together with the names of other entertainers on posters at upscale places like the Billy Rose's Diamond Horseshoe Club, Betsy's favorite performance venue because it is closest to the apartment.

Luckily Betsy does not have to face the hardships and pitfalls of many other girls who work in New York without a parent or guardian to provide food, shelter, and security. As for her mother, Blanche is happy to have developed new friends among the tight-knit Jewish community of New York, which provides a degree of stimulus to offset the boredom of waiting for Betsy to return to their modest flat from rehearsals and performances. On the whole, both mother and daughter were content with life as the United States slowly recovers from the Great Depression that had devastated people all over the world.

There are, of course, times when Betsy is unable to find work, so she alone or the two of them take little holidays to various New England towns and waterways that are quite different from Texas. By then Betsy has obtained her driver's license, making it easier for them to get around.

Live entertainment at the many social clubs in cities around the United States would almost always feature professional singers, and might often include talented dancers like Betsy as well, who could do high kicks or tap dancing with ease. If the available dancers still had their youth and shapely torsos like Betsy's, they would invariably be dressed in skimpy costumes to entice men at the bar to keep ordering more drinks.

After being on stage for ten to fifteen minutes, dancers needed a break from the exertion of their routines, so a comedian or perhaps a vocalist might follow their acts. On a typical evening, the dancers might do two or even three performances to earn their keep, after which they would go back to their tiny apartments or shared dormitories at the YWCA, or perhaps go out for a late evening date with a friend. In Betsy's case it was usually back to her mother, but that pleased her because they were both happy with each other's company, and they very likely shared the role of "being in charge." Choreographed dancing was an arduous occupation, but for Betsy it was a constant thrill to be in New York City after growing up in the small Texas town of Seguin.

Then suddenly everything is shattered by the awful news from Pearl Harbor in Hawaii, thousands of miles away. As more bad news filters in over the following weeks, and people realize that Japan is intent on conquering Singapore, Hong Kong, the Philippines and other places, panic well and truly sets in for the people of New York and other big cities on both coasts of America as rumors circulate that they could be next to get bombed.

Somewhere in January or February '42 as the war news worsens, and as soon as Blanche is able to terminate their furnished apartment contract, she and Betsy return to Seguin where they are fairly certain the Japanese will not bother them. Blanche goes ahead by train while Betsy waits for a promised rental car to bring all their luggage, though she leaves her dancing costumes at the Diamond Horseshoe.

It is getting dark by the time Betsy reaches Tennessee and she suddenly finds the highway blocked. This causes her to turn into a little dirt road that eventually leads into a pasture where there are lots of men milling about. One man in particular seems to be the most important, so she gets out of the car and approaches him, then tugs at his sleeve. He turns around and looks at her incredulously before bellowing:

"WHO THE HELL ARE YOU AND HOW IN HELL DID YOU GET HERE?"

After the grouchy man tells someone to "get her the hell out of here" and—after looking Betsy over a second time—for the someone to "get the hell back here double-quick," Betsy learns that the grouch is General

George Patton. He and his army were on maneuvers in preparation for their eventual assault in Europe!

Betsy is still twenty-two when she arrives in Seguin with the car. In spite of the Pearl Harbor shock she is already feeling independent and wants to help her mother with expenses, so Betsy gets herself a job at the Fort Sam Houston motor pool in San Antonio, driving munition trucks at first like other women. Eventually she is promoted to delivering the mail. Her helper is a little old black man whose job is to load and unload the heavy mail sacks, and who normally rides in the back with the mail. On one particularly hot day Betsy asks him if he wants to ride up front in the cab where it is a bit cooler, and he is happy to do so. At the end of that day Betsy gets called into her boss' office to be told she has been seen with a black man riding in the truck with her, and if that happens again she will be fired.

Betsy's response was, "Sir, it definitely won't happen again because I quit!"

After things in the Pacific seem to have quieted down—when the Battle of the Coral Sea in May of '42 shows that Japan's thrust across the Pacific has been blunted—Betsy goes to her wealthy Uncle Julius in San Antonio and asks him for money to go back to NYC and start a serious career. She tells him not to worry, as she knows how to deal with men. Apparently she does because he gives her the money for living in New York, this time on her own.

Betsy has her heart set on doing Broadway shows instead of cabaret dancing this time. She starts auditioning soon after finding an apartment and getting a telephone installed, both of which were expensive propositions. Betsy soon realizes she will be broke in three months even with the kind donation from Uncle Julius. She urgently needs to find a roommate to share the apartment expenses but can't think of anyone she can trust that much. In desperation she telephones Blanche in Seguin.

"Momma, I need some help. I am auditioning and think I will soon have a job on Broadway, but I need a trustworthy girl to help share the apartment expenses. The rents and telephone are much higher now than when we went back to Texas just a few months ago. I guess the war is doing that."

"But honey, you know I can't afford to help now that Papa's alimony has run out," Blanche responds. "You also know I had to sell our beautiful house on College Street, that was designed by the famous architect Atlee Ayers. Sugar, you'd better go find that roommate, a nice girl like you ... but wait, I have an idea, you know? Just the other day I ran into my cousin Mrs. Otto Blumberg; Olive is her name, remember?. Perhaps you also remember her daughter Valerie who was a year behind you in school? Yes? Well Valerie heard about you being in New York and asked her momma whether she could take dancing lessons too. Apparently the girl has been working in San Antonio for the past four years as a secretary, but doesn't like that kind of work at all. I'll bet if I tell Olive that you have an apartment and will look after Valerie, that Olive will let her go to New York for a few months to take lessons, and you could probably suggest a good teacher for the girl. It would help with your rent and other expenses too. What do you think?"

Betsy is astonished that her problem might be solvable after all. She practically drops the phone.

"Oh Momma, that would be perfect!" Betsy shouts with the receiver upside down. Please go see Mrs. Blumberg tomorrow, or maybe tonight."

"What, dear? I couldn't hear you. Say it again, a bit louder."

"Oh Momma, I'm so excited. This will be a perfect solution, at least for a few months until I start earning. Or maybe Valerie will want to stay in New York for years, like me!"

So it happens that Betsy gets a phone call one July afternoon from the Greyhound Bus terminal. It is Valerie Blumberg, who sounds exhausted and on the verge of crying.

"Don't get upset, girl. Just get a taxi and give him this address, then come up to the second floor when you arrive. I'll keep an eye out for you in about half an hour, OK? Hurry now, before it gets dark."

Almost thirty minutes later, the doorbell rings and there stands a very disheveled but smiling brunette from Texas, with a fancy leather suitcase beside her.

"Lordy, Valerie, you look a mess. Here, give me your bag, and I'll run you a bath. Grab that bathrobe by the door and get out of those dirty clothes this minute. And give me a shout when you want me to scrub your back. Wash your hair first, though," Betsy orders."

When the ablutions are completed and her new roommate is seated comfortably in an arm chair, Betsy passes her a sandwich and begins an interview.

"First of all, you need a new name for theater work. Like my full name is Elizabeth but that's too long for billboards so I use Betsy, which was also my Seguin nickname—and I have a stage surname too, which is Berkley. So I'm Betsy Berkley when I'm in New York, see? Well, Valerie is almost short enough, but what did your friends call you at school in Seguin? I don't remember you very well, 'cause I left after my junior year and that was ages ago, but you look nice and slim enough for dancing."

"They called me Val, and some Seguin people still call me that, Betsy, but I really prefer to keep Valerie even though you're welcome to give me a stage surname. And I remember you, though, since you were a year ahead of me. We're about the same size now, I guess. You're so nice to let me share your apartment. Momma would never have let me come to New York otherwise. And she asked me to give you this," handing Betsy an envelope full of cash.

"Oh my goodness, Valerie, that's really kind of your mother. We can sort out the finances—and your stage name—later, 'cause I need to ask you some more questions tonight, OK?"

Valerie nods, and Betsy proceeds.

"Valerie, this is a very personal question and I need an honest answer if we are to get along well together. Have you ever, you know, done it with a man before?" Valerie shakes her head, looking embarrassed, so Betsy asks again: "Honey, it's OK to tell me. Have you even seen a naked man before?"

"Oh Betsy, of course not, except ... well, during high school in Seguin, I, um, well, one day, this guy and me; he was a friend in my class, and we had a, um, a class field trip and we, um, snuck away from the rest of the class and, um, well, we took off our clothes by the Guadalupe River where there is a little boat dock, and, um, jumped in and splashed around then kind of, um, you know, cuddled and played with each other's, you know, bodies."

Valerie looks at the floor, but when Betsy laughs out loud at the story, so Val starts laughing too.

'Then what happened, sweetie? Wait, let me get you a class of water."

"Well," the girl goes on, gulping the water, "our teacher Miss Grey had been looking for us, and she suddenly jumps out from behind a tree—I guess she was watching what we were doing—and she insists we get out of the water and put on our clothes right there in front of her! I was really too ashamed, but he—my friend—went ahead and did what she asked, and I still remember that his, um, his thing was really stiff, and he had trouble getting his shorts on, so Miss Grey went to help him. She maybe had a towel or something, 'cause she was rubbing him all over before she pulled up his shorts. Anyway, I quickly climbed out of the river and soaking wet got my bra and panties and other clothes on when they weren't looking, and I ran back home to Momma. Well, it was a long time ago, but I'm still embarrassed to think about it, especially because I was I was only fifteen at the time."

"Wow!" Betsy exclaimed, "I bet the teacher took that boy home and played with him some more. Did you ever talk to him about that day?"

"Well sure, and I think you're probably right," said Val. He would never tell me what happened, but one day after we went on that field trip I heard him and a couple of other boys laughing and kind of singing to each other after Miss Grey's art class, "Hey, hey, Bridgit Grey, what'll we do to get an A," so I guess she was playing with several of the boys in our junior class, and maybe some seniors too. She was fairly good looking and just out of college, though I thought she was plump and overweight."

"That's a really funny story, kid. But I'll ask you again—have you ever really done it with a guy?"

"Well, no, and I wouldn't know what to do, exactly, but why do you ask?"

Betsy explains: "because I don't know either and I don't intend to find out until I get married. Val, you'll find lots of temptations here in New York, and you need to be on your guard all the time. You're very pretty. Men will flirt with you, and some will ask you out, and some may even force you into a corner and try to pull up your skirt. No matter how polite they are or aren't, they all want the same thing, to get into your pants. It's a lot rougher here than Seguin or San Antonio because so many girls let themselves go just to get a job on stage. Men in the theatrical world expect to get what they want, and most of the time they succeed."

"Betsy, thanks for telling me all these things. I'll be on my guard, and I've had to chase off a few guys in the San Antonio office where I worked, so I'm not a stranger to harassment. Let's just be good friends and watch out for each other. And thanks again for sharing your place with me."

"No problem, babe. We can watch, and wash, each other's backs, for sure," Betsy jokes, looking very relieved, "I'm really glad that we're on the same page. Tomorrow I'll take you to the dance studio and introduce you to my former teacher. She is a whiz; I can tell you. Now let's get some sleep."

Three happy months pass while Valerie grows to love her dance lessons and Betsy finally gets hired in a Broadway show. That show is still running when Valerie brings up a subject that Betsy had completely forgotten about.

"Betsy, my three New York months are almost up, and I'm supposed to go back to Seguin. Momma even bought me a return ticket for the bus when I came up here. I kind of don't want to go back unless you want me to. I've been thinking about all this for some time, and I would love to stay here with you and do some Broadway dancing together. Would you let me do that?"

"Sure I would, kid, but what about your parents? Will they let you stay longer in New York?"

"I think they would have no objection considering that I am now twenty-one," Valerie said, "and they might even advance some more funds—although I may have to go back and negotiate that part. Mainly I wanted to see if you are willing to put up with me for a while longer."

"Heavens yes, sweetie, I've grown quite fond of you, especially when you get up early and fix breakfast! Kidding aside, I would miss you if you left me alone, so go back and work on your parents and let's get it settled."

Soon afterwards, Valerie goes to Seguin to see her family, and Betsy's first Broadway show winds down after 40 weeks. When Valerie calls her with the good news that her parents will fund her for another three months to see if she can earn her own living, Betsy announces that a new show is coming up for tryouts in two more weeks.

"Hey, hurry back here girl, and let's do these tryouts together as the Texas Showgirls," Betsy says happily, "and by the way, I've been thinking about your stage surname. How does Valerie King sound? They don't really want more than four syllables between the first and last names."

"Great! I like it! And I'm coming back fast—by train this time, would you believe?"

Both girls are hired for a show called *Vickie* that opens on September 22nd at the Plymouth Theater and runs for five weeks with 48 performances. They are both exhausted after the cast party.

"Hey Val, I've been thinking," Betsy says after they get home, "It's really not fair of these companies to ask the cast to rehearse for two weeks without any pay and expect us to live on their crummy salaries if a play folds up in, say, three or four weeks. I say let's agitate for a union so that people will get paid for rehearsals too. What do you think?"

"Mmm, maybe so," Valerie replies, "But we probably won't get hired any more if we start that sort of thing."

"I know, so what we'll have to do is broadcast the idea all over town and get people to walk out of rehearsals now and then, until we get the production companies—one at a time—to agree to a vote. I think maybe a good union might help us with funding if they see we're committed to going down that road."

Betsy's plan bears fruit after a few months, because even some company directors feel that they have been mistreating the cast members all along. Betsy writes excitedly to her mother about the good news and her achievement with the union.

In their triumph, Broadway shows continue for Betsy Berkley and Valerie King during the last half of 1942 and all of '43. It is during those tense wartime days that several of their friends get married and invite the Texas Showgirls to many a modest wedding ceremony. Sadly, however, some of the marriages seem to end in less than a year as one or another of the couples divorce and wander off with other partners or become casualties on some far off battlefield.

This gets Betsy wondering about her parents' divorce when she was five, but she never discussed such things with Blanche when they were together off and on during those prewar years in New York. Now she wishes she had, which starts her writing regularly to her mother, a habit that she continues all through the war years and beyond. Betsy adored Blanche, whom she would describe to friends as "a real lady, and a southern belle."

Then in January 1944, Betsy's life is to change though it isn't obvious at the time. Both girls' first Broadway job that year is dancing in the chorus of Mike Todd's musical comedy *Mexican Hayride*, which opens at the Winter Garden Theater on January 28th and is to run for over a year. It has a slightly spicy theme that garners a lot of attention from the public, and eventually from a new civic group called the United Services Organization.

The USO, as it is more popularly known, was formed in early 1941 at the suggestion of President Roosevelt, to help lift servicemen's morale in the face of lonesomeness and anxiety from many hard and bloody battles being fought around the world. Co-sponsored by half a dozen existing civic groups such as the YMCA and the Salvation Army, the USO was an umbrella organization that partnered with the War Department to provide hospitality and entertainment to the Armed Forces at home and abroad.

The initial USO activities were hospitality-related, whereby some 3,000 service clubs were eventually opened all over the United States, staffed by volunteer hostesses (and chaperones) in order to give servicemen a safe and wholesome place to relax off duty. Most of those clubs were just coffee bars, but some larger ones would also host dances on weekends, which Betsy and Valerie would attend from time to time.

Not long after the clubs were started, the USO Camp Shows were launched. The overseas Camp Shows—also known as "the Foxhole Circuit"—were aimed at entertaining the GIs who were away on active duty overseas. Individual performances by such popular comedians as Bob Hope and Jerry Colonna or Laurel and Hardy, or singers like Marlene Dietrich [who was also an OSS operative—Ed.] provided highly popular entertainment at the larger military and naval bases in both the European and Pacific Theaters.

By 1944, larger and larger shows were heading overseas, and one of those was—you guessed it—Mike Todd's *Mexican Hayride*, which was

*Hope and Colonna in '42*

shaping up to become one of that year's super-successful Broadway shows, particularly since it had very little to do with Mexico. Casting eventually consisted of three troupes so that one of them could go on the road in the US, another one would always be available on Broadway, and finally—because of the USO—a third troupe could go overseas to entertain the troops.

Betsy volunteers to be in the USO troupe—and chuckles when they are made to clean up the dialogue—but Valerie chooses to stay behind with the Broadway troupe because she is still afraid to leave the United States and her parents.

But we are getting ahead of the main story—World War Two in the Pacific Theater. A great deal of action is still to take place between June 1942 and June 1944 when Betsy Berkley and the *Mexican Hayride* troupe are suddenly sent to Hollandia, New Guinea to entertain MacArthur's new Army. Mike Todd's cast of men and women—who had already been practicing the show at East Coast Army camps, having been promised that the USO would send them Europe—get packed into a former Matson liner, SS *Monterey*, with their custom-tailored woolen uniforms to wear in the tropics! The ship also carries several other USO Camp Show casts, dozens of Red Cross workers, and three platoons of nurses, so it was definitely crowded (and definitely chaperoned!).

## *\*\*\* THE NATIONAL DRAFT \*\*\**

An impeding 1940 nationwide draft, recently signed into law, and a rush to avoid it by joining some preferred branch of the services in advance, prompts some young men of draft age—such as Clarence Saegert, working on his Bachelor of Science degree at the University of Texas—to choose the Navy Reserve in which to enlist. Patriotism was part of Clarence's motivation, but he also needed a way to avoid the draft while completing his university degree requirements. Belonging to a reserve organization would keep him at home, Clarence assumed, and he fancied the Army or Navy over the Marines.

In 1940, Clarence's father, the stalwart Seguin High School principal known as "Papa Joe Saegert," was pressuring him to join one of the services while he was in college, so Clarence tries the Army but is rejected for poor eyesight. Soon afterwards, Papa Joe gets after him again to join up, so Clarence, who has a phenomenal memory, memorizes the entire standard eye chart that the services use. When the examining doctor says aloud or taps the chart at something like Line 3, 5th letter, Clarence replies from memory and is soon accepted into the Navy Reserve. No one ever finds out about his myopia before he is back home in 1945 from a year's active duty with PT Boats in the Pacific.

### *** SEMPER FIDELIS ***

But many other young men do choose the United States Marine Corps after the draft law comes into effect. Skinny twenty-year-old twin brothers from Norman Oklahoma named Alex and Ajax Jones decide to sign up at the Marine recruiting office in Oklahoma City after a big party at their mutual girlfriend's home in Norman. Well, Mabel Fisher isn't really a girlfriend of either twin, let alone a fiancée, yet they are both in love with her but haven't been able to get the pretty debutante to choose between them, in spite of each having (at first unbeknownst to the other) made a proposal of marriage on bended knee.

The twins are not identical, but both are quite handsome. At 5' 11", brown-eyed Alex is slightly taller than Ajax and he bears a small scar on his cheek from a fishing trip when their dad accidentally bumped Alex out of the rented boat while hauling in a big bass from the river mouth in Louisiana where they went on vacation. As he fell overboard, Alex cut himself on the cheek with the scaling knife he was holding.

"Hot damn," exclaims Ajax, his light blue eyes watering from anger after they both storm into the bathroom of their university dormitory in order to talk privately. "That girl is so damned stubborn I reckon neither one of us will get to marry her."

"Yeah, that's right," Alex replied, "I bet she has some other idiot on the string and is just jerkin' us around in case that guy doesn't come through with a proposal."

"You're exactly right, Bro, let's just forget about Miss Mabel and activate our backup plan for getting a draft exemption—by joining the friggin' Marines!"

The twins were both sophomores at the University of Oklahoma (OU) but were not doing very well that year because of the many distractions including football (at which they both excelled) and girls (at which they didn't), and because of the international military situation that everyone was constantly talking and worrying about. In 1940 and '41, America was officially a neutral nation, but things in Europe were "hottin' up" as Germany rolled over one country after another, and there were occasional rumors about a possible war in the Pacific one day too, because German commerce raiders had been encountered here and there from South America to the mid-Pacific.

After carefully withdrawing from their OU classes so they could return one day and pick up where they left off, and after bidding farewell to their parents, early November 1941 finds the twins on a train to California, cracking peanuts and shooting the breeze with groups of other people around their age, male and female. Occasionally the train would stop in places like Albuquerque New Mexico and Phoenix Arizona where passengers were allowed off for 30 minutes to stretch their legs or buy things from the station kiosk, while the coal-burning engine took on more water for making steam.

Neither Alex nor Ajax were smokers, but on the train there were several passengers who did smoke and who encouraged non-smokers to try a puff. Before long there were more neophytes than acolytes of the smoky vice, including both the twins and several flirty young women. The closer the train came to Southern California, the more profitable the station kiosks became, and the more often pairs of young smokers sneaked into the communal bathrooms in their carriages, but not for a smoke.

Eventually the pleasant three-day trip comes to an end, and reality sinks in for the Jones twins and no doubt for others as well. Alex and Ajax find there are a few other Marine volunteers disembarking from the long train, and their little group is soon herded outside the station to where a green open-backed truck awaits. Some members of the group have longish hair, but most are sporting crew cuts like the Jones brothers, probably inspired by the smartly turned-out recruiting sergeants that signed them up.

"Get your sorry asses aboard, you people," a veteran Marine corporal growls, his barracks cap displaying the Marine Corps globe-and-fouled-anchor insignia. "You're gonna regret you ever left home and your dear old mommies. Now get a move on there, just heave your stuff up and climb on up after it! We've gotta get movin'—NOW!"

Confusion reigns as the dozen or so people all try to lift their bags and suitcases at the same time, until Alex jumps up onto the truck bed and tells the others to wait their turns and pass their things to him one at a time. Ajax quickly joins him and begins stacking the luggage forward behind the cab. The angry corporal, who is rolling his eyes at the pandemonium, pauses and asks the twins for their names. They both smile and jump down from the truck bed to reply:

"Er, I'm Alex Jones and this here is my brother Ajax," was the answer. What's your name, um, Corporal?"

The response is immediate: "My name is Sir, not Corporal, not Corporal Sir, but just plain Sir, and don't you forget it, shitbirds. You are lower than whale shit to me, and so is the rest of this fucked up bunch of yo-yos. Now get your asses aboard with them, and I want you two shitbirds to report to me after we get to your new home, the Marine Corps boot camp, understood?"

"Yes, um Sir," the twins mumble in unison.

"What? I can't hear you!" the corporal yells.

"Yes, Sir!" the twins repeated. "Louder, and the rest of you people too!" comes the order.

"YES, SIR!!

"That's more like it," the corporal continues in a normal voice. "Now listen up: whenever you are spoken to by anyone of a rank higher than shitbird, sound off loud and clear, got it?"

The truckload of "boots" nod as one, and yell again together: "YES, SIR!

"Alright, all aboard," the corporal tells the driver as he hops into the cab. The truck lurches forward, and the twins' new lives begin.

There are some smirks, but no one riding in the back says a word as the truck proceeds away from the station for some twenty minutes and is then waved through the main gate of a manicured-looking facility not far from the San Diego Airport, to the right side of which is a long row of attractive two-story Spanish-style white stucco buildings with red curve-tiled roofs and a handsome covered walkway with arches. Out of the corners of their eyes, some of the recruits spot the large red sign outside the entrance as they drive through, that states in impressive gold letters:

### UNITED STATES MARINE CORPS RECRUIT DEPOT
### SAN DIEGO CALIFORNIA

Later they will learn that there is a similar MCRD facility at Parris Island, South Carolina, for recruits from the eastern region of the US. (*Verbal rivalry was well-entrenched, with California recruits calling the others "Swamp Rats" and being themselves called "Hollywood Marines"–Ed.*). Much sooner than that revelation, however, the truckload of new recruits learns that the nice Spanish-style buildings inside MCRD San Diego are not for them, as the vehicle turns left and comes to a stop at a row of old two-story brown wooden barracks with tin roofs. There is a huge asphalt-surfaced parade ground near the barracks, what Marines call "the Grinder,' and in the near distance they can see rows of odd-looking smaller huts with rounded roofs and no visible walls, that are corrugated outside. They later learn that those strange buildings are newly-invented Quonset huts for an expected larger influx of recruits, and that the old wooden barracks will soon be torn down.

The twins also learn that Marine lexicon is laced with (among other things) everyday naval terms such as "scuttlebutt," "the head," "the deck," "the bulkhead," "ashore," "aboard," "ahead," "astern," "belay that," "fore and aft," "the galley," "the mess hall," etc, and that Marine detachments serve aboard Navy ships to provide security, while the Navy in return provides Marines with medical services ashore and in combat, where medical technicians known as "corpsmen" accompany Marine units into combat, wearing Marine uniforms with Naval insignia *(in the Army, corpsmen are called medics – Ed.)*

Any "boot " heard calling his rifle a gun is forced by his DI to stand in front of the platoon and—holding his rifle in one hand and his penis in the other—to recite in a loud voice: "This is my rifle and this is my gun; one is for fighting; the other's for fun."

When the Pearl Harbor news reaches MCRD San Diego on Sunday morning December 7th, 1941, it almost creates a riot, so eager are the recruits to get over to the Pacific and "beat the shit out of those damned Japs." Well, the Jones brothers and their platoon still have to go through combat training at Camp Elliott before they can be assigned to an active Marine Corps division for overseas deployment, although the rumor is that it will be the First Marine Division for them, known as "The Old Breed" because it was the first such organization of that size in the Corps, although there is also a Second Marine Division in formation. *(By the end of WWII there will be six of those Marine divisions in combat – Ed.)*

## *** CLEANING UP THE MESS ***

The City of Honolulu Hawaii was not as heavily damaged by the recent Japanese raid to the extent of the nearby Pearl Harbor Naval Base, but there were the occasional piles of rubble to dispose of in the city. Civilian, Navy, and Army work parties soon clean up the city, while their unluckier brethren toil many long hours trying to restore the battered naval facility to a semblance of its former self. It was a thankless job but little by little the important base and anchorage began to function again.

Meanwhile, crews of experienced ship builders, marine engineers, and specialist construction workers from all over the United States, started the enormous task of refloating the damaged ships. Two of the battleships were clearly beyond salvaging, the *Arizona*, and the *Oklahoma*. Some others had settled in the shallow harbor without capsizing, and were refloated first, along with three cruisers and several destroyers that had also been sunk. Capsized vessels were more difficult to deal with and were left until last. Several damaged ships that were still afloat were prioritized in the Navy dry docks, one of which had itself been targeted.

While the cleanup went on, it became obvious to almost everyone that Japan must have spies in Hawaii who told them where to find this, that, and the other important targets for bombing and strafing.

One afternoon, Bongo Perkins meets with Admiral Brady and his staff to discuss how to go about finding those spies without actually rounding up and incarcerating all people of Japanese ancestry in the islands, as the FBI had recently suggested in very strong terms. The admiral speaks:

"Commander Perkins, I would like you write up a summary of this excellent meeting for my eyes only and deliver it to my office within the next 48 hours. Meanwhile, kindly have your assistant take action to see that US Immigration is preventing people from leaving these islands by sea or air, until we issue further instructions. I think the suggestions that were made here today are quite good, and that we need to implement them as quickly as possible. The rest of you officers are hereby excused but you are forewarned that no mention of today's discussions shall leave your lips—or else! Carry on, Perkins."

"Aye, aye sir," Bongo responds, collecting his papers and hat. He stays in his quarters that evening, to ponder the recent events and think about what to write for Admiral Brady. Upon learning that senior Japanese Admiral Yamamoto was behind the horrendous attack on Pearl Harbor, he tries to project himself into the mind of that shrewd warrior whose profile he had studied at the Navy Staff College.

Having also been somewhat trained to read the three intermixed Japanese written languages, Bongo notices from the ancient script known as *Kanji* (in which educated Japanese names are written), that Admiral Yamamoto's peculiar birth name Isoroku (五十六) simply means "56," apparently because the admiral's biological father had sired him at that advanced age. He further ponders the fact that the shrewd attack on Pearl Harbor took place when the admiral himself was 56 years old. Bongo's strange brain would often come up with odd thoughts like that whenever he was enjoying his favorite after-hours beverage, Old Orkney scotch whiskey.

## *** JAPANESE AMERICAN INTERNMENT ***

Naval and civilian leaders in Hawaii respond to the US government's order to intern all Japanese Americans by saying that it is an impossible task in view of limited manpower and the many islands that would have to be secured and monitored. President Roosevelt agrees with them, and they are exempted, but the US Army and the FBI on mainland America pursue the restraining order with great gusto. Eventually, by February 1942, some 120,000 people of Japanese descent were forcibly rounded up and sent to camps in the western interior states. Around two thirds of those men, women, and children were American citizens, but that important fact was overridden by their racial makeup.

Meanwhile among the Hawaiian Islands, martial law is put into effect, together with a 10 pm curfew. Some internments do in fact take place, but selectively not universally. A dragnet operation based upon the admiral's recent staff meeting yields promising results through the efforts of several anonymous informers, and the civilian police are directed to make nearly two dozen arrests using warrants issued by the Shore Patrol.

Local banks are required to have their stock of US dollars overprinted with the word HAWAII and people are only allowed to draw out $200 worth per month. Any person spending cash that is not overprinted would be arrested for questioning.

## *** OUT WITH THE OLD ***

Around that time, heads are beginning to roll among the former leadership of the Pearl Harbor facilities, starting with Vice Admiral Husband Kimmel and Lt. General Walter Sharp, the former naval and military commanders, who are both relieved of command on December 17th. Admiral Kimmel goes first, even though some people thought the surprise Japanese raid was not really his fault. His replacement as Commander-in-Chief of the Pacific Fleet (CINCPAC) is Admiral Chester Nimitz of Fredericksburg Texas.

Admiral Nimitz takes command of the Pacific Fleet in a ceremony aboard the submarine USS *Grayling* (SS-209) on December 31st, 1941, with his predecessor Rear Admiral Kimmel in attendance—having been recently reduced from vice admiral—standing with Major General Short, who had likewise been reverted to his former rank

Nimitz tries to reassure Kimmel that "it could happen to anyone," but the fact remains that neither Kimmel nor Short had understood or reacted seriously to the various warnings that drifted their way from January 1941 onwards, nor had either of them made a point of studying

Photo # NH 50799   Adm. C. W. Nimitz on board USS Grayling, 31 December 1941

the historical tactics of Japan from when it defeated the Russian fleet in 1904 until more recently when Japan gradually pocketed important coastal regions of China. Unfortunately, therefore, Hawaii in 1941 was under the care of two solid traditionists in great need of strategic staff members or better yet, the wisdom of an old Asia-hand mentor.

As Admiral Nimitz begins interviewing his inherited staff members and department heads in mid-February, it is soon the turn of Rear Admiral Ronald Brady who is in charge of the PT Boat squadron and the Office of Naval Intelligence, about which his contemporaries often queried him over the unusual combination. Admiral Nimitz is particularly interested in the ONI's role or lack thereof in the recent Pearl Harbor disaster.

"Admiral Brady, please tell me why the commanders of this important base were not properly alerted as to Japanese intentions, seeing as your records show several warnings were received here from British and Australian sources over the previous six months."

Ronald Brady coughs and shifts in his chair, having asked himself the same question numerous times over the past three weeks.

"Sir, I cannot fully answer that question except to say that the credibility of those few sources was questionable. They were mostly civilian observers of typical unreliability—such as alcoholics or adventurers who were living with, and even married to local women—and who were categorized in our records as fabricators of tall tales and fictional events. Our protocols against which we measured those few alerts invariably coded them as unreliable—I am very sorry to say in retrospect."

"So how do you feel about our impeccable Navy protocols now?" Admiral Nimitz asks his perspiring subordinate. "Give me at least one good reason why I should not ask you to fall upon your sword, so to speak, and please be quick about it."

"Sir, I cannot condone my own interpretation of what has turned out to be invaluable evidence that we ... that I ignored or downgraded. Honestly, I was actually laughed at by both commanders and all of their staff members, in fact."

"None of whom had paid any attention to the writings of Somerset Maugham," Admiral Nimitz interjected. "Admiral Brady, I sense that you have learned a valuable lesson from those Japanese bombs and torpedoes that violated the supposed sanctity of the white man's refuge at Pearl Harbor, am I right?"

"Oh yes sir, indeed I have had a rude awakening, and I shall never again underestimate the cunning and tenacity of oriental races, that I swear."

"You are forgiven, Admiral Brady, and please do not again ignore the decades-old intuition of so-called rum-soaked planters and castaways in the Pacific region. Many of those men are fearless and loyal beyond belief. An Australian naval person is at this very moment organizing those stalwart gentlemen into a network of what he calls Coastwatchers, who will need to survive by extreme cunning behind Japanese lines throughout the many islands that we will need to reconquer before this war is over, and their very lives will depend upon the loyalty that their native populations will hopefully show them, because there will be heavy wireless gear to carry and weapons as well, not to mention food and water. You are dismissed, sir."

"Aye, aye sir; thank you, sir," is Rear Admiral Brady's relieved response, as he recognizes his new boss to be a man of shrewd intellect and deep wisdom—or was it the other way around? At any rate, he resolves to probe the racial prejudices of his own staff, beginning with Commander Bongo Perkins in the absence of Commodore Stanley "Stoney" Wall, director of his ONI branch. *Damn, why did I let Stoney go on leave at this time? Anyway, he and the PT Boat division can wait until a later date.*

"Perkins, I would like you to meet me at the club this evening at 1700 hours," Admiral Brady growls into the telephone as soon as he reaches his office.

When Bongo and the admiral are seated in a quiet corner of the Navy O-Club and are taking their first sips from the drinks that have just been delivered, a familiar voice interrupts their meditations.

"Good evening, one and all. What's this I hear about a war with Japan?"

Bongo rises with a smile to shake hands with his direct boss, Commodore Wall, who is supposed to be on leave in the US. Admiral

Brady is also surprised, but happy that he can now deliver his lecture to both senior ONI officers together.

"Grab a drink, Stoney," the admiral says, reaching over to pull up another chair. "We didn't expect you back until after New Year's."

"Yessir, that was the plan, but when we heard about the Jap raid I figured I'd better get out here fast or be kicked out of the Navy. Is Admiral Nimitz still on the warpath?"

"Yes he is, but I've already had my whipping and now it's my turn to jump on you two. Get your drink first, Stoney, and then we'll begin. Bongo, take a few notes please."

All ears, the commodore and the lieutenant commander are told about Admiral Nimitz's lecture on the value of listening carefully to any and all sources of information that might come from British or Australians through unofficial channels, and particularly from civilians who have lived in the Pacific for generations and who could probably guess better than the Americans what the Japanese were likely to do next. After their discussion, the admiral asks Commodore Wall to remain a while longer but speaks to Bongo as well.

"Commander Perkins, I'm told by Captain Silvers, our ONI contact on Admiral Nimitz's staff, that a British civilian named Perry will arrive tonight aboard the Coast Guard cutter *Taney* with a secret message for—well probably for all of us. I would like you to meet with this fellow tomorrow evening at, say, the Moana Hotel, and see what he knows that we could act upon. Better let Captain Silvers know where you'll be meeting after Perry gets through paying his respects at Pearl. This fellow could be a shining example of what we have just been discussing."

"Certainly, sir. I didn't realize *Taney* would be back here so quickly after the Jap raid."

"Yes, she didn't go far after the raid, only to Canton Island and back. That's apparently where the Englishman came aboard. Alright, off with you now so I can finish bringing your boss up to speed about all the recent events."

## *** THE VIEW FROM SINGAPORE ***

Berthed at Singapore's world-famous naval base were two recently arrived capital ships that had been sent out by British Prime Minister Sir Winston Churchill to help deter Japan from going to war. They were a recently commissioned battleship HMS *Prince of Wales*—aboard which Churchill and Roosevelt had met in August off faraway Newfoundland—and an older battlecruiser HMS *Repulse*. They reached Singapore with four attendant destroyers, but without an intended aircraft carrier that had accidentally run aground in the Caribbean, and without the customary two or three cruiser escorts either. Upon arrival, their Admiral Tom Phillips promptly rushed off to Manila to confer with American Admiral Thomas Hart, who was in charge of the US Pacific Fleet.

When the City of Singapore was raided and bombed by Japanese planes from Saigon Indochina on December 8th, the newly arrived warships and the naval base itself were not seriously threatened, much to everyone's surprise. A few weeks later the reason becomes crystal clear—Japan wants an intact naval base for its own use and intends to capture it intact!

Before the four destroyers and their two special wards sail forth from British Naval Base Singapore late in the afternoon of December 8th, intent on intercepting a Japanese invasion force, they are given the identity code of *Force* Z. Near sundown on the 9th, *Force* Z is east of Kota Bharu in northern Malaya, but not having found any evidence of enemy landing forces, Admiral Phillips decides to bring the fleet quickly back south to the safety of Singapore, unaware that his ships have been sighted earlier by a Japanese submarine.

Around midnight, as the weather clears and a bright moon lights up the seas, they are sighted by another Japanese submarine that immediately reports the British fleet's position. The following morning, wave after wave of Japanese planes suddenly deliver their deadly "fish" with practiced accuracy, first at the *Prince of Wales* and soon after at the *Repulse*. The big ships are clearly doomed as groups of torpedo bombers continue to attack them from alternate sides in spite of their twists and turns and heavy anti-aircraft fire.

It is *Repulse* that first sinks below the waves, and soon afterwards the *Prince of Wales* begins to founder. Not much later, the surviving crews of both ships are swimming. The destroyers manage to collect some two thousand officers and ratings from the sunken capital ships, but not all swimmers are so fortunate—among them Admiral Phillips, the fleet commander. Thus ends the Battle off the Malay Coast, as the Japanese quickly name their brilliant achievement *(that foretells the obsolescence of battleships in general – Ed.)*.

It turns out that the Japanese do not invade Malaya directly but instead land at Singora in southern Thailand on 8 December 1941, moving almost immediately across the Thai-Malay border to capture a nearby RAF air base in northern Malaya.

For the next two months, British and Indian troops fight a losing battle against a tough Japanese army led by Lt. General Yamashita Tomoyuki, as brilliant a strategist on land as Admiral Yamamoto is at sea. General Yamashita's outnumbered but better trained troops keep up their pressure on the Allied defenders, allowing them no chance to rest and reorganize, instead pushing them steadily southward down the Malay Peninsula toward Singapore.

British planners had counted on the thick Malayan jungle to help stop any invaders, but the Japanese are skilled in jungle warfare and use their knowhow to continually outflank the British who are forced to retreat down the roads.

The leading Japanese soldiers confiscate hundreds of bicycles from local Malayans, and pursue the retreating British at a fast pace with this unorthodox tactic. The bike riders push on even after the tires wear off their machines. The collective rattling noise from the bikes panics the Indian soldiers, who assume they are being pursued by tanks!

Singapore is an island separated from the southern tip of Malaya by a shallow and fairly narrow waterway known as the Straits of Johore. Across this waterway is a man-made causeway that provides road and rail connections between the two colonies. After crossing over to Singapore, the retreating British troops dynamite a huge gap in the causeway that temporarily causes the Japanese to halt and regroup for a week near the town of Johore Bahru on the Malayan side.

Not far from the eastern side of the dynamited causeway, a small islet called Pulau Ubin lies in the center of the Johore Straits. Because this little island could theoretically mask the approach of the Japanese in small boats, Lt. General Arthur Percival, the Allied commander, concentrates the bulk of his British and Indian troops along the Singapore shore that flanks the island. At the swampy shore on the other side of the causeway he stations his smaller group of Australian soldiers under the command of their Major General Gordon Bennett.

On 8 February 1942, General Yamashita lands his troops on the west side of the Causeway, in the sector where the Australian division is scattered in the swampy ground among various rivers and creeks. Although the Australians fight well, Percival neglects to reinforce them, still believing that a larger Japanese attack will occur near Pulau Ubin to the east.

Once Japanese troops are across the waterway, there is heavy fighting in all sections of Singapore Island. With air superiority, and heavy artillery being brought over the hastily-repaired causeway, it is just a matter of time before Yamashita demands an unconditional surrender. When Percival finally gives in to this demand and surrenders his forces, he is unaware that Yamashita's troops are almost out of ammunition and food, and might have been defeated after all.

*Japanese Troops Enter Singapore City*

# CHAPTER TWO

## *** JAPAN ON A RAMPAGE ***

*4th Marines on Corregidor 1942*

*Corregidor Surrenders*

## *** GUAM AND WAKE ***

After receiving the news of Fortress Singapore's ignominious defeat, British Prime Minister Winston Churchill is stunned by the loss, calling it the greatest British defeat in history; but there is equal tragedy ahead for the Americans as Japan tallies up victory after victory on land and at sea.

The stunning defeat of the British at sea—the *Force Z* disaster off Malaya—is also a harbinger of obsolescence for the world's battleship fleets and their many admirers, designers, and builders, who gradually realize that air power has come of age and the most important naval vessels from that point forward will probably be aircraft carriers and submarines.

On December 10th, while the Battle off the Malay Coast is already in process three time zones to the east, a Japanese Army regiment, whose transports are supported by four heavy cruisers, comes ashore on Guam in the Marianas with negligible resistance from the small Marine detachment stationed there that has no heavy weapons. The Mariana Marines were primarily in Guam to make certain that Pan American Airways passengers are safe when their seaplanes dock offshore for refueling.

In centuries past, Guam was a reprovisioning stopover for Spanish traders whose sailing ships traveled back and forth between Acapulco in Mexico and Manila in the Philippines. Guam, an approximate halfway point, was the southernmost and largest island of a north-south crescent-shaped island chain that the Spanish named Las Marianas in the 16th Century, after Queen Maria Ana of Spain.

Ironically, when the Pacific War broke out in 1941, all other islands of the Mariana crescent including Rota, Tinian, and Saipan, had already been under Japanese custodianship for some twenty years. Those former German colonies—and several others in the Pacific region—had been awarded to Japan at the end of the First World War, following Germany's defeat.

Germany had previously bought all of the Mariana chain from Spain in 1899, following Spain's defeat in the Spanish American War, but after losing the First World War, Germany's Pacific colonies were confiscated by the League of Nations. The entire Mariana chain was offered first to the United States, but Guam was their only island of interest at that time, partly to support forthcoming civil aviation, hence Japan was able to claim the large remainder—a blunder that the US was soon to regret.

When Japanese forces moved ashore on Guam in December 1941, its capital city Agaña had already been bombed (unnecessarily) by planes based in Saipan, a mere 150 miles away. It seems peculiar in retrospect that the United States did not militarize Guam much more extensively, given the nearby Japanese presence. Unsurprisingly, the Japanese conquest of Guam was easily accomplished before the end of December, with the assistance of Japan's Saipan colonists.

The next day, however, Japan suffered its first defeat of the Pacific War when it attempted to subdue tiny Wake Island, located eastward of Guam towards Midway and Hawaii. Like Guam, Wake's small atoll was also established by Pan Am as a refueling stop for its pioneering seaplane network that connected Hawaii with the Philippines, Hong Kong, and Singapore.

The Japanese knew that Wake had minimal defenses, and their bombing raids the day before destroyed Pan Am's facilities and the Marine barracks. The Japanese admiral in charge of the invasion fleet felt confident of victory after learning that Guam was likely to be an easy task. His resources consisted of two destroyer-transports and two troopships, protected by three light cruisers and six destroyers. A landing force of 450 naval infantry prepared to go ashore, but this time the defending US Marines had half a dozen 5-inch coastal defense guns with which they managed to damage all three cruisers and sink one of the destroyers, resulting in the invasion fleet withdrawing to Kwajalein whence it had come. Four still flightworthy Marine fighter planes of VMF-211 that survived the prior day's Japanese bombing raid, pursued the retreating Japanese ships and managed to sink another destroyer.

The stout defense of Wake Island hardly compensated for US losses at Pearl Harbor, but it was nonetheless something positive for the Allies to cheer about. Wake requested immediate reinforcements to forestall a renewed attack, but further help could not reach them before the next Japanese landing succeeded in overcoming the defending Marines and taking control of the base.

## *** HONG KONG AND MACAU ***

Japan also invaded the British Colony of Hong Kong on 8 December 1941, the same day that Pearl Harbor was attacked on the other side of the International Date Line. Because the colony was vigorously defended by British and Canadian troops, Japan's treatment of captured women, children, and wounded soldiers was brutal and barbarous. Many of the wounded were slaughtered in their hospital beds, and nurses were raped and killed as well, sometimes on top of the hospital corpses. Civilians were also treated with callous disregard, and crying children were often shot just to silence them. Hong Kong officially surrendered to Japan on 25 December—Christmas Day—a bittersweet outcome.

Japan did not invade Macau, a Portuguese colony that was also situated in the Pearl River estuary not far from Hong Kong, ostensibly because Portugal had declared its neutrality and was to remain neutral throughout the war. Instead they forced Macau to accept Japanese "advisors" who were there to keep an eye out for any signs of belligerency.

### *** THE PHILIPPINES **

When news of the Pearl Harbor attack reached the Philippines early on the morning of 8 December 1941, US aircraft were launched at daylight from Clark Field on Luzon to search for an invasion force, but finding nothing they returned to refuel and prepare for a night attack on Formosa, from where an invasion would logically come. Late that afternoon as American planes were being warmed up for their night time sortie, Japanese bombers arrived to destroy most of them on the ground in spite of radar having detected the incoming planes. That tragedy was the opening salvo of a four-month battle to defend the Philippines, led initially by General Douglas MacArthur until he was directed by FDR to escape with his family and staff by PT Boat to Mindanao, and then by B17 bomber to Australia.

After a four-month series of retreats, first to Luzon's Bataan Peninsula and finally to the small island of Corregidor, US forces finally surrendered, and the survivors were either imprisoned or sent to Japan as slave labor. A lengthy Bataan Death March to Camp O'Donnell of over 60,000 US and Filipino prisoners bore further testimony to the brutal tactics used by Japanese invaders. A significant number of captives were bayoneted if they dropped by the side of the road from exhaustion.

### *** BONGO GETS HIS ORDERS ***

While the US Army and Navy in the Philippines are still battling Japanese invaders, Bongo and the Englishman Peter Perry meet for dinner in Honolulu and again the next day at the Botanic Gardens to discuss the strange secret which Perry brought with him—that Japan had almost finished constructing the first of four enormous battleships with 18-inch guns, the largest warships and guns that the world had ever known. Apparently the first of those IJN monsters, named the *Yamato*, was ready for sea trials, and the second one—as yet unnamed—was fairly well along also.

"This is totally bizarre, Peter, you would think those huge ships could bankrupt Japan, along with the cost of their war in China and now their attacks against us and our allies."

"They must be counting very heavily on capturing the Dutch East Indies oil and so forth," Peter replies.

"Of course you are right, but their emperor must be quite fanatical to take such huge risks. We will eventually defeat them, of course, though it may take several years. Anyway, Peter, I must leave you soon as I have just been posted to Australia to set up an ONI branch and am looking for transportation to get me to Sydney."

"Congratulations Bongo. I've been searching for a ride to Sydney also, where my wife and son settled after leaving Singapore, but Captain Silvers says the only thing available this week is a PBY to Canton Island and Fiji. At least that will get me closer to them, and I wouldn't mind stopping at Canton Island again, having spent a month working there last year."

'Well, I don't want to get stuck out there in the middle of nowhere, old sport, so I guess this is goodbye. It has been a great pleasure to know you, Peter."

"Likewise for me, Bongo. Perhaps our paths will cross again one day."

Their paths cross sooner than expected. Peter is lounging inside a Navy PBY Catalina seaplane the following afternoon, awaiting takeoff, when in crawls Bongo Perkins with a Navy-blue duffel bag and a broad grin on his face.

"G'day Peter, here I am to keep you company all the way to Canton Island and Fiji, after which we shall both be in the market for a Sydney Express."

"Good grief, you turn up like a bad penny, as the expression goes, but no offense intended. Well, there are no actual seats to offer you, so pull up a bit of floor and soft luggage. I'm told we shall be lifting off in about twenty more minutes."

After the liftoff, both travelers manage to fall asleep as the two-engine PBY drones westward through the night. At some point the copilot wakes them to partake of sandwiches and coffee.

"Six more hours to target, gents. If you need to go, there's a bucket in the head over there," pointing to a small cubicle.

"Where in the world are we now?" Bongo asks.

"Mmm, I could give you the coordinates, but they might not mean much unless you are a navigator. Let's just say we're about halfway to Canton Island from Pearl, flying roughly southwest. If you drop off again, I'll wake you once we get close. I have to take over from the skipper now. Bye"

"That's fine, and thanks for the chow," Bongo mumbles with a mouthful of spam and cheese. Peter nods his thanks also.

"Got anything to read, old sport?" Bongo asks Peter after they finish the welcome snack.

"Ha. Who could read in this vibrating machine?" Peter replies, "but I do have a story for you about these Phoenix Islands, if you're interested."

"So try me, Limey pal; give it your best." Bongo changes position among the duffel bags so he can hear Peter better.

"Alright then. I'm certain you know about Amelia Earhart's tragic demise in 1937, but are you also aware that she was headed for an island called Howland that is quite close to Canton Island where we shall soon arrive?"

"No, I am not aware of that, and I have never heard of Canton Island either. I thought maybe it was near China," Bongo chuckles.

"Nothing to do with China, old geographer. We shall soon be touching down in the Phoenix Islands, which are about halfway between Hawaii and Fiji. Both Howland and Canton are part of the Phoenix Group"

"OK, now I'm calibrated," Bongo confesses. "But what about Amelia?"

"She was accompanied by Fred Noonan, supposedly the best navigator of Pan American Airways that built all these bases across the Pacific. Pan Am volunteered Noonan to help make certain that Amelia reached her rendezvous with your US Coast Guard cutter *Itasca*, that was already at Howland Island awaiting her flight."

"Now that you mention it, I do remember that Noonan was involved with her disappearance," Bongo says, trying to sit up among the duffle bags that practically fill the PBY hold. "Do you think he screwed up?"

"Possibly," Peter replies "but nothing is certain about their disappearance. However, a British official from Tarawa in the nearby Gilbert Islands, was visiting all the Phoenix islands in the early 1940s as part of his job, and he discovered some human bones and a few artifacts on Gardner Island, another Phoenix Island (*modern day Nikumaroro – Ed.*) not far from Howland. He sent those things to Fiji for analysis, but with the war starting out here recently the samples have disappeared, just like Amelia herself, although the bone analysis report was recently found."

Bongo then becomes very interested. "And?" he prods.

"Aha, you are finally awake," laughs Peter. "Well, the analysis confirmed that the bones were from a Caucasian human but little else, however it does make one think that Amelia and Fred may have run out of petrol and crash-landed near Gardner, although no trace of the plane has been found there. Amelia's last recorded transmission to *Itasca* showed that they were flying on a sight line that would intersect Howland, but apparently they overflew the cutter in bad weather or else they were already past Howland before they started the search—and ran out of fuel, perhaps just off Gardner Island. It is very sad in either case."

Just then the copilot opens the cockpit door and announces that they will be splashing down in the Canton lagoon within thirty minutes. Bongo and Peter gather their things in silence.

## *** ALLIED PREPARATIONS ***

As bleak as things look for the US and its allies after the concerted Japanese attacks on Hawaii, Hong Kong, Malaya, Singapore, the Philippines, Guam, and Wake Island by early 1942, the Allies nevertheless prepare to retaliate. Using Melbourne Australia as a transit point, the large French colony of New Caledonia with its capital Noumea is gradually militarized by three Army National Guard infantry regiments from North Dakota (the 164th), Massachusetts (the 182nd), and Illinois (the 132nd), with orders to defend New Caledonia

Under the watchful eye of Major General Alexander Patch of the regular US Army, the three disparate Guard units get rigorously trained on New Caledonia during the summer months of 1942, with the intention of being combined into a combat-ready Army infantry division. To be known eventually as the Americal Division from its five-month association with New Caledonia, the new infantry division is soon to exceed expectations.

Meanwhile the First Marine Division under Major General Alexander Vandegrift is readied in California for a strike against some still unspecified Japanese holding in the Pacific. Known as "The Old Breed" because it was the Marine Corps' original fighting force, its three infantry regiments are the 1st, 5th, and 7th Marines, plus the 11th Marines artillery regiment *(although not all of them were available for the landing – Ed.).*

Attached to Company A, First Battalion, 5th Marines (1/5) are the twin Jones brothers, Privates First Class Alex and Ajax, fresh from intensive infantry training at Marine base Camp Elliott north of San Diego *(the much larger Camp Pendleton having not yet been activated – Ed.).*

The twins received their meritorious promotions to Pfc (Private First Class) upon graduation from boot camp in San Diego three months before, having served as Right Guide (Alex) and Left Guide (Ajax) of their platoon because of their initiative in loading some new recruits and baggage at the San Diego railway station the previous year. A right guide's responsibility in boot camp was to assist the platoon's drill instructor (DI) with military training and weaponry classes, and it was the right guide who carried the platoon's guidon, or pennant, at the head of a platoon when it practiced complex marching in formation.

A left guide was responsible to the DI for the platoon's administrative records, plus assigning other recruits to after-hours guard duty known as "fire watch." The left guide marched at the very rear of a boot camp formation; hence he was the last member of a platoon into the mess hall for meals. If he was a smoker, this individual would learn to eat very quickly in order to find time for a cigarette while most of the platoon was already forming up for a march to its next instruction site and a lesson in, for example, disassembling and reassembling its World War One bolt-action rifles.

After boot camp graduation, new Marines were first sent to Camp Matthews for rifle marksmanship qualification, then to Camp Elliott near San Diego for combat training, which involved live firing at simulated enemy roads and towns, although Camp Elliott was hard pressed to create a simulated Pacific jungle. Nevertheless those who passed the combat training courses were quite eager to put their new skills to work, even though the First Marine Division had not yet received any orders as the month of May 1942 rolled around.

"Hey Bro, what's the scoop about when we'll be shoving off for somewhere?" Alex asks his brother Ajax who is once again involved with administrative duties, this time for their company commander. The brothers have arranged for a weekend liberty pass together in mid-May for the first time in five weeks, and are waiting at a bus stop outside the base for a ride to San Diego, some fourteen miles away. They look carefully around before speaking.

"No idea at all. Nobody seems to know what's in store for us grunts, but there are plenty of rumors bouncing about," Ajax replies. "And there's also some hot scoop about somewhere else."

"Somewhere else—hey that's where we're going, right? Somewhere else."

"Very funny. Listen up, comedian. There was a big naval battle last week, what they're calling the Battle of the Coral Sea."

"Where's that," Alex asks, "this Coral Sea?"

"Heck, I don't know, but it's out there in the Pacific somewhere. Apparently the battle went on for a week or so. We lost the carrier USS Lexington, and the Yorktown was also badly damaged but made it back to Hawaii.

"Holy crap, that means we don't have any battleships after Pearl Harbor, and half our carriers are out of action, right?"

"Well, yes, but the Japs lost a light carrier, and their two fleet carriers had to retire like our *Yorktown* did, because of damage.

"So what does that mean for us?" Alex asks. "Anyway, here's the bus. We can talk about this later on."

When the brothers get back to Camp Elliott after a rousing weekend in San Diego where they enjoyed meeting some cute Mexican girls and learning a few new tricks, there is much more buzz in the camp about the Coral Sea battles. Ajax updates Alex after chow the next evening. They are both in Company A but are separated into different platoons.

"Alex, the Coral Sea is southeast of New Guinea, which means a bit north of Australia where General MacArthur is getting his act together. Apparently the Jap carriers were guarding an invasion fleet heading for New Guinea's capital, Port Moresby. The Aussies were garrisoned at the port, and their cruisers helped us with the naval battles. After that the Jap invasion force turned back and left the scene, so I figure we did make some brownie points in spite of losing the *Lady Lex*."

"Man, this is great to hear," Alex replies excitedly. "It means they won't be invading Australia any time soon. But what about us—the First Marine Division?"

"Patience, Bro. I see some top brass visiting the division HQ more and more often, so I reckon we are due to ship out pretty soon. It's almost the end of May and we've been picking our noses here for a month or more, so surely Roosevelt wants us out of here and earning our keep somewhere else."

"There you go again, Bro—somewhere else. We should write a song about that place."

## *** THE DUTCH EAST INDIES ***

After Germany occupied the Netherlands in May of 1940, forcing the Dutch government into exile in London, and Japan launched its multipronged attacks upon British and American colonies in December 1941, the colonial Dutch government in Batavia made efforts to coordinate with British, Australian, and American naval forces in a futile attempt to deter Japan from conquering the Dutch territories in the Pacific and seizing their vital oil and rubber production. An Allied organization known as the ABDA (American British Dutch Australian) Command was patched together in the hope that Japan could be thwarted, but the lack of prior fleet exercises to develop a common communications protocol meant that the effort was doomed to failure. By March 1942 Japan was in control of

Borneo, Java, and Sumatra, and the world's fourth largest supply of crude oil. Much glee was shared at the Emperor's palace in Tokyo.

Japan had planned for several years to take control of these oil-producing territories that would also provide rubber, tin, and other strategic products to sustain its long war with China. Up to then, the main supplier for Japan's oil was the US, an ally of China that was vigorously protesting Japan's belligerency. When Japan also gained access to strategic harbors and airfields of Vichy French Indochina, the US promptly cut off oil supplies to Japan. This abrupt US embargo was supported by British and Colonial Dutch governments as well.

Japan then had only two choices; to back down and stop its war with China, or to press on and seize the oil-rich territories that it coveted. It chose the latter path, but to protect itself from military intervention by the US and its allies, Japan needed to strike first by crippling the US, British and Dutch resources, and then conquering sufficient territory in the Pacific to protect its gains. Its empire-building plans were grandiose and complex, but it counted on negotiating a truce that would leave it in control of those critical resources.

## *** MEANWHILE BACK AT THE RANCH ***

One of Betsy Berkley's 1942 trips back to Seguin to visit her mother, Blanche Seligmann, happened to coincide with a former classmate Clarence Saegert's Spring Break holiday, a ten-day relaxation that was hugely popular with university students. By accident they meet at a grocery store one morning, where both were shopping for their respective parents.

"Hey there, Betsy," Clarence shouts and waves as he heads into the grocery just as she is coming out. "Where the heck have you been hiding?"

"Oh Clarence, how great to see you again," Betsy replies smiling as she stops to put down her shopping bag and shake hands. Why, I've been in New York since '36, working in Broadway shows. Didn't you know?"

"I had no such idea. Is this your first time back to Seguin? I always wondered what became of you when you didn't show up for our senior year at SHS."

"No, I come back every two years at least, and Momma comes to see me in New York too. I got the show biz itch during our junior year and just had to go to the Big Apple and get started dancing. What are you doing these days?"

"I'm still at UT Austin and in the Navy Reserves too. I've been married since 1940 to Evelyn Gartman, but I reckon the Navy'll send me overseas one of these days.

"Is she from Seguin?" Betsy asks. "I don't remember that name. Anyway, congratulations, old buddy."

"Thanks Betsy. No, Evelyn is from Austin. Well, my dad is still Superintendent of the Seguin schools and he's expecting me home with some breakfast makings while I'm here on Spring Break, so I'll have to run and do the shopping now. It really is great to see you after so many years, Betsy, and after so many years together at school too. I guess the Saegert and Seligmann alphabet kept us sitting together from way back there in Kindergarten," he chuckles.

"Yep, that must have been it," Betsy agrees. "Well, the world sure has changed since those old days. Take care of yourself and your wife, Clarence. I wish you both the best of luck."

"You take care too, Betsy." And they go their separate ways, not imagining a future meeting in the Pacific war zone.

## *** THE NEW HEBRIDES ISLANDS ***

In 1906, the New Hebrides islands to the northeast of New Caledonia became a British-French Condominium, a rare situation whereby two colonial powers agreed to jointly administer a single colony. In reality, though, the many individual New Hebrides islands were only rarely co-governed. British governance took place in some of the islands, and French governance in others, with the respective local populations being taught to speak the appropriate colonial language in addition to their own native dialects. A rare linguistic exception was the island of Efaté, seat of the condominium's capital in Port Vila, where English and French were both taught.

Somehow everything worked well in those idyllic islands until World War Two broke out in the Pacific. At that point, the British representative wielded more power than his French colleague because of France having been conquered by Germany. As a result, the Allies were given access to specific (mostly French) places on several of the islands, such as Savannah Bay on Efaté and an area near Luganville on Espiritu Santo where the Allies were allowed to develop military and naval bases, hospitals, and airfields. Why the Allies—and particularly the US—needed these new bases close to Australia was soon to be revealed.

HMAS *Adelaide* off Port Vila in 1940, courtesy of Stan Billington

# CHAPTER THREE

## *** STEMMING THE TIDE ***

*Battle of Midway Warmup*

After the Battle of the Coral Sea in May 1942, there was a glimmer of hope that Japan's aggressive behavior could be stopped. With overall US control and the support of the US Allies Australia and New Zealand, the Pacific Theater was divided into two administrative sections under General MacArthur based in Brisbane Australia, and Admiral Nimitz based in Hawaii. As might be expected of an Army leader, MacArthur's area, the

Southwest Pacific (SWPA), comprised the larger island land masses like New Guinea, Java, and his beloved Philippines, and he was also in charge of most US Army forces in the Pacific.

Nimitz, being Navy, had lots and lots of smaller islands and a great deal of empty ocean assigned to him. Although MacArthur had his own Navy too—the US 7th Fleet under Admiral Kinkaid—Nimitz had a much larger fleet, known alternately as the 3rd Fleet or the 5th Fleet, including all the large new aircraft carriers and his own landing force, the US Marines. His armada was commanded alternatively by Vice Admirals Halsey and Spruance, and the Nimitz area of responsibly became known as the Pacific Ocean Area (POA).

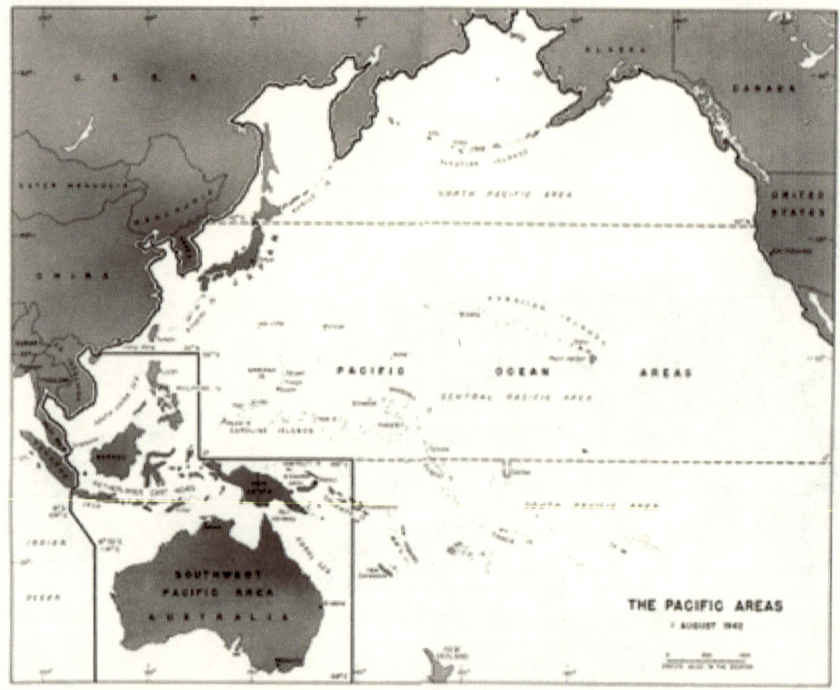

Meanwhile, in spite of its setback in the Coral Sea, Japan was still bent on following an original plan that envisaged capturing Midway Island, and the eventual invasion of New Caledonia, Fiji, Samoa, and the New Hebrides islands.

Midway was next on their list.

## *** THE BATTLE OF MIDWAY ***

Japan's next thrust against the United Sates began—oddly enough—with an invasion of the Aleutian Islands Attu and Kiska off Alaska in June 1942. After the shock of having their homeland bombed by carrier-launched B25s in April, the Imperial Japanese Army (IJA) wanted to capture the Aleutians to prevent another bombing by way of the Arctic circle. Meanwhile—a day late on June 4th in coordinating with the IJA strike in Alaska—the IJN Combined Fleet, under the overall command of Admiral Yamamoto once again, began to attack Midway Atoll, which had been set up by Pan American Airways as its first refueling stopover after Hawaii, on the way to Wake, Guam, and Manila. Four of the original six carriers that launched the Pearl Harbor attack were again under the command of Vice Admiral Nagumo, and those four would lead the attack at Midway.

This time the Americans were ready, as they had broken the Japanese code and were able to figure out that Midway was the target of an imminent attack.

Soon after Midway-based Marine fighter planes incurred heavy losses while attacking the incoming Japanese fleet, planes from US aircraft carriers *Enterprise* and *Hornet* under the command of Rear Admiral Raymond Spruance, skillfully engaged the Japanese carriers, sinking three of them. Sinking the fourth enemy carrier was credited to aircraft from the *Yorktown*, which had been hastily repaired after the Coral Sea battle in May, but *Yorktown* was later damaged and sunk as the Midway episode came to an end. Nevertheless, Midway was overall a great US naval victory that helped stem the tide of Japanese aggression.

Further help was soon to come from the First Marine Division, led by Major General Archer Vandegrift in the British Solomon Island Protectorate.

## *** TULAGI AND GUADALCANAL ***

Activities by both Japanese and American forces were generally quiet during the month of July 1942, as both adversaries rushed to rebuild and reallocate their resources. During this break, commercial vessels from Canada and the US were able to supply Australia and New Zealand with troops and equipment.

However, air reconnaissance showed that the Japanese were building a seaplane base near Tulagi, a small but important island in the Solomon Island group that Japan had captured in May from British plantation owners. Further inspection showed that Japan was also constructing an airfield on Tulagi's nearby large island of Guadalcanal. The latter observation served to activate—at long last—an assignment for the First Marine Division which was forming up at Wellington New Zealand toward the end of July. In Able Company, First Battalion, 5th Marines (A/1/5), the Jones twins were busy packing their gear for an expected action somewhere in the Pacific.

"Well here we go at last, Bro," says Alex when they are able to meet up for a cigarette break after their company commander was called to battalion HQ for a meeting. "One of these days we'll find out where Somewhere Else is really located."

"You still on that kick?" Ajax chuckles, cleverly rolling a cigarette with a gadget that he bought in the PX. "Well, I already know that we're going to some place in the British Solomon Islands, smart ass. And there are lots of Japs there. Don't shoot yourself in the foot when we load in the Higgins Boats to go ashore."

"Well, ain't you the smart one, eh? But you weren't smart enough to get us some time away from this New Zealand base so we could check out the town. Hell, the only Kiwi women I've met are the old ladies that serve our chow line in the mess hall.

"Ha; just don't get down on your knee and ask one of them to marry you, dummy, 'cause the skipper won't sign your papers."

Alex grins and shoots back: "So how could you know that, Bro? I guess you already tried to marry one of those old ladies yourself, right? Uh-oh, here comes the Cap'n now, and it looks like he's heading our way. Better get rid of these cigarette butts."

"Jones and Jones," comes the order as their company commander grows closer. "Go tell your platoon leaders that we'll move out at 0600 tomorrow with full equipment, and there'll be a briefing after noon chow today at 1330. Also tell them we'll be at sea for about five days, got it?"

"Yessir; aye, aye sir," the twins snap to and salute.

As 1/5—the First Battalion 5th Marine Regiment—lands on Guadalcanal (code-named CACTUS) less than a week later on 7 August 1942, there is virtually no resistance from Japanese troops, the reason being that Japan had no advance warning of the US invasion. Their people were mostly airport workers, who high-tailed it into the bush where they hoped someone would send for help. Help did arrive the next night in the form of a fleet of Japanese cruisers and destroyers.

On Tulagi, a small island across the wide channel from Guadalcanal, it was a different story.

Tulagi—sheltered in the bay of a larger island called Florida—was where British plantation administrators and their families had been living in a mosquito-free environment, and where a native black man would stand out like a sore thumb. Tulagi—abandoned by its British and Australian overseers before the Marines arrived—is also where Japanese troops had decided the previous May to set up their headquarters for a seaplane base. The base was fully operational many weeks before the US invasion fleet arrived. In fact, it was their seaplane activity that had attracted the attention of Allied scout planes to Tulagi, and those scouts had also reported the airfield being constructed on the big island of Guadalcanal.

Tulagi in turn had two small subsidiary islets called Gavutu and Tanambogo that were joined by a man-made causeway, where the Japanese float planes were tethered. Japanese troops were well dug in at all three locations, and when the Second Battalion 5th Marines (2/5) went ashore at Tulagi, they were soon caught in the middle of a fierce firefight. So was a smaller detachment of Marine Raiders that went ashore on Tanambogo near the Japanese seaplane ramp.

Meanwhile, two battalions of the 2nd Marine Regiment went ashore at each end of the Florida Island bay to flush out any Japanese that might be guarding Tulagi's flanks, but none were found. The 2nd Marines were part of the Second Marine Division that had been lent to "The Old Breed" for the Tulagi invasion.

On Guadalcanal itself, the troops of 1/5 moved cautiously westward along the coast to take up their bivouac at the mouth of a wide creek. The nearly-completed Japanese airfield was not far from the other side of that creek.

By nightfall on August 8th, Marine landings had prevailed and all those islands were secured, with very few enemy prisoners being taken. However, the Allied warships that were protecting the Marine transports and supply vessels were about to get a bloody nose. Near the center of the 20-mile-wide wide channel that separated Guadalcanal from Florida Island—with Tulagi sheltered in its bay—there was a small uninhabited island called Savo that looked vaguely like a circular cone on maritime charts. Around this cone, the Naval Battle of Savo Island was about to begin.

"Holy crap, look at all the lights!" shouts Pfc Alex Jones, who is on nighttime guard duty near the shore of Guadalcanal. Many others of 1/5 get awakened by gunfire from ships that seem to be rushing back and forth while shooting at each other.

The Sergeant of the Guard joins Alex by the shore. "Where the hell is our artillery? We could probably pop off some of those ships if the 11th Marines wake up and get moving!"

"Yeah Sarge," Alex agrees excitedly, "but how could they tell which ones are Japs?"

As the naval battle rages on in the darkness, broken intermittently by gunfire, searchlights, and overhead flares—and some of the ships are hit and set on fire—the Marines on shore feel a deep frustration at not being able to help their Navy comrades. When dawn comes on the 9th, the Marines gradually learn that the US Navy was badly defeated in the previous night's ferocious battle.

"It looks like we lost four cruisers last night, Bro," Ajax tells Alex when they meet up for noon chow in the Able Company mess tent. A ruddy-faced corporal named Bridgewater from Ajax's platoon overhears the conversation.

"Where did you hear all that stuff, Jones?" he asks. "You make it sound like a friggin' disaster!"

"Well it was a disaster. I heard about it at the company HQ, Corporal," Ajax answers.

"OK, OK, but don't bother calling me Corporal. I may be an NCO but we corporals still have to eat with you grunts. Besides, we're in a combat zone now, so ranks are not so important. Just call me Billy, OK?"

"Sure, Billy, but the naval battle was definitely a disaster for our fleet," Ajax repeats, "and I heard that we have no air cover now so they're going to pull the transports out tonight."

"No shit," said Alex, "they are nowhere near unloaded! Billy, I'm this smart guy's brother Alex, from Second Platoon. Glad to meet you."

Corporal Billy Bridgewater shakes hands with both brothers, saying: "Looks like we're stuck here then. Better tell your buddies to start diggin' holes and stringin' barb wire. Don't wait for an order from the boss."

"Yeah, you're right. OK, see you later, Billy." And the trio hurry off in their separate ways.

Around mid-morning on the 9th, a bleary-eyed collection of senior Marine officers, hastily summoned by the campaign commander Major General Alexander Archer Vandegrift, are huddled in a morning downpour to assess the situation. Learning that the aircraft carriers were withdrawn, thereby depriving the invasion force of air cover, the group does not blame the partially unloaded transports with their battered remaining escorts from likewise planning to retire from harm's way the following night. The question for the weary Marines is what they can best do to defend their positions and prevent further gains by the Japanese.

"US and Australian sailors have just learned the hard way that Japan's expertise at night battles is far better that their own," the general states.. "By skillful use of cloud cover by day, Admiral Misawa's task force of cruisers and destroyers was able to move up here and then sneak around the south side of Savo island in the black of night to devastate the ships guarding our transports, launching torpedoes and firing heavy deck guns with precision, then crossing the channel to batter our other ships defending the Tulagi contingent before disappearing back around the north side of Savo."

The First Marine Division normally comprises the 1st, 5th, 7th, and 11th regiments, but the 7th Marines were still in American Samoa where they had been sent soon after Pearl Harbor, and a battalion each from the 1st, 5th and 11th Marines were across the wide channel (which was christened "Iron Bottom Sound" that morning by some clever person), guarding Tulagi. That left General Vandegrift with only four battalions at hand on Guadalcanal itself, plus some howitzers and a company of light tanks.

Most heavy artillery weapons were still aboard the transport ships, as were other critical things like extra ammunition, clothing and food, but Vandegrift's Marines vowed to hold onto their gains at all costs. The first step was to move everyone westward across Alligator Creek to form a wired-in periphery east and west of the airfield, and from the north shoreline into the hilly jungle at the south.

"Hell, I just about finished digging my foxhole," Ajax complains to Billy Bridgewater as word comes for the battalion to pack up and move across the creek, which involves struggling upstream through brambles to where the waterway is crossable, and doubtless having to dig another hole somewhere else.

"Well, would you rather be part of the detail that has to move all our supplies across that creek to the new location? I can arrange that for you, no problem," the corporal responds. "Or maybe you can help the guys who are filling in the shit trenches and digging new ones."

"Aw, come on, Billy, don't be a hard ass. I didn't mean nothin' by it."

After Billy's platoon hacks its way across the upstream water crossing on the airfield side, they are told to go way on past the airfield and then dig in on the west side of the new perimeter, down by the shoreline again. Normally the senior NCO of a platoon is a sergeant, but Billy is temporarily in charge of Able Company's third platoon while his platoon sergeant is on recon around the airfield with a work party to bring over the Japanese stores that were left behind by the workers who fled into the hills. Among the stores are canned foods and bags of rice that help make up for the supplies that sailed away with the Navy transports.

"How old do you reckon this rice is, Billy?" asks Alex Jones as he stares at the gooey ladle-full that a messman has just sloshed into his metal dish after he stood in line outside the hastily-erected mess tent. "You reckon it's OK to eat this stuff?"

"Of course it is, dummy. Don't you know that rice is like red wine; the older it gets the better it is and the more valuable. I learned all about rice from my pappy in Louisiana."

"No shit, Dick Tracy," another Marine comments, "I heard that eatin' rice makes your skin go yellow like the Japs."

"No way, Jarhead, that's what Atabrine does, and you'll be getting' a dose of that as soon as my buddy the corpsman gets unpacked," adds one of the Navy boat drivers.

Several other Marines in the chow line laugh at the discussion.

"Shut your face, swabbie, or I'll fill it with this gooey crap!"

"Okay, okay everybody, calm down," Billy the corporal shouts. "Either you eat the rice or you starve. I'm telling you it's fine to eat rice, no problem-o. Ain'cha heard've Kellogg's Rice Krispies?"

Further on west of 1/5 in the new Marine enclosure, the River Lunga flows steadily toward Iron Bottom Sound and discharges its waters via several tributaries. In between this river and Alligator Creek that the division just crossed from the east, Marine engineers struggle to complete the captured air field using abandoned Japanese equipment and manual labor. By August 12th the basic work is completed and the dirt strip is declared suitable for fighter aircraft. The airfield is christened Henderson Field on that day, in remembrance of the Marine Air Wing squadron leader, Major Lofton Henderson, lost in the recent Battle of Midway. A few days later, the first Marine and Navy fighter planes are flown over to CACTUS, to the cheers of the beleaguered Marines in their foxholes. From that point on, those daring flyers become known as the Cactus Air Force (CAF).

### *** THE LONG HAUL ***

Henderson Field and its Marine defenders are located centrally along Guadalcanal's north coast, and thus unable to prevent the Japanese from landing troops at both ends of the 90-mile-long island in order to attempt its recapture. Although Major General Vandegrift does move the Second Battalion 5th Marines (2/5) over to Guadalcanal from Tulagi, continued pressure from Japanese infantry build-ups and their sleep-depriving air patrols each night are gradually wearing down the fighting edge of his understrength Marine division. Foreseeing an eventual crisis, Vandegrift urgently requests that his missing 7th Marine Infantry Regiment be relieved from guard duty in American Samoa and sent to Guadalcanal as quickly as possible. His request is granted, with the 7th Marines due to arrive by mid-September together with a missing battalion of the 11th Marine Artillery Regiment, but they do not arrive in time to avert a near disaster.

While the airfield with its daredevil CAF fighter squadrons is defended at the waterfront and both sides by regular infantry battalions, the inland jungle side is allocated to the Marine Raider and Parachute Battalions under Lt. Col. Merritt "Red Mike" Edson. A long treeless ridge extends into the jungle and it is along that ridge and its flanks that Edson deploys most of his forces.

Late at night on 12 September, an uncoordinated Japanese attack takes place, that is beaten back by Red Mike's defenders. The following night, however, a full brigade of screaming Japanese soldiers with fixed bayonets boils up from both sides of the ridge to engage the Marines. Fierce hand-to-hand combat ensures, but the Marines are carefully drawn back toward the airfield by Edson via successive defensive positions, with the result that nearly 600 Japanese are killed and the remainder slink away with their wounded. The Battle of Edson's Ridge—also known as Bloody Ridge—goes down in history and Red Mike is awarded the Congressional Medal of Honor for his skillful handling of the potential disaster.

Five days later the 7th Marines arrive from Samoa, to hoots of derision from their veteran comrades.

"Where the hell have you guys been?" someone shouts as the 7th Marines march up from the landing beaches.

"Where are you going next?" yell some others.

"Tokyo," answers their famous regimental colonel Lewis "Chesty" Puller. "You fellows coming with us?"

## *** THE AMERICAL DIVISION ARRIVES ***

In mid-October 1942, the 164th Infantry Regiment of the Americal Division arrives on Guadalcanal as the first US Army unit to see combat in either the Pacific or European theaters. The 164th is a former National Guard regiment from North Dakota that was extensively trained on New Caledonia together with its companion regiments the 182nd from Massachusetts and the 132nd from Illinois. The 164th's baptism under fire occurs two nights after arrival on Guadalcanal when the Marine perimeter in which it is situated comes under intense bombardment from two Japanese battleships that cruise up and down Iron Bottom Sound while pounding the target area with their 14-inch guns. Some CAF planes are destroyed on the airfield and several Army and Marine casualties occur also. Over the next few days, the 164th is gradually integrated into Marine tactics and helps repel repeated Japanese counterattacks later in the month.

Due to transportation scarcity, the other two Americal regiments arrive piecemeal during November. Being armed with the new M1 Garand semi-automatic rifle, the Americal regiments cause many casualties among the Japanese that constantly try to storm the wired-in airfield perimeter. A Marine staff sergeant—John Basilone—is awarded the Medal of Honor for staying alone with his machine gun throughout the worst Japanese attack to date. Bodies are found strewn around his position when the attack is finally beaten off.

"Jones, where the hell did you steal that M1 rifle from?" Corporal Billy Bridgewater demands of Pfc Ajax Jones when the dawn light shows hundreds of dead Japanese outside of and tangled across the barbed wire that surrounds the Marine perimeter.

"Aw come on, Billy. You know darn well I didn't steal it. One of those Americal guys got hit last night in the Banzai charge, so I figured I could do more damage with his M1 than my old '03. Some other guys in our platoon already got one for the same reason."

"Hell, that's OK then. Them fellas from the 164th did a helluva job to help us, that's true. I heard that the general even calls them the 164th Marines now! Well, better keep your '03 too, in case we have an inspection one of these days, OK?"

Ajax nods and chuckles to himself, remembering that some of his squad are referring to Billy as "Corporal Bilgewater" behind his back, because of his fussy ways. The fact remains that dead or wounded Army troops get quickly relieved of their M1 rifles by envious Marines who gladly put aside their old '03 bolt-action weapons from the First World War.

## *** THE NAVIES FIGHT ON ***

After the disastrous Naval Battle of Savo Island when US Marines first arrived on Tulagi and Guadalcanal, and after the October shelling of Henderson field by Japanese battleships, two more massive clashes at sea take place during November 1942 as the Japanese attempt to bombard Henderson Field and put ashore large numbers of troops. Both those night actions, are collectively known as the Naval Battle of Guadalcanal, and each of them demonstrates, once again, the Japanese superiority with nighttime tactics. Although the Americans achieve a tactical victory in the end by preventing the destruction of Henderson Field and the landing of

Japanese heavy equipment and troops, those actions are a tremendous cost in terms of US lives lost and ships sunk.

The final clash even involves battleships firing at each other for the first and only time anywhere in WWII. Each side loses one of them in that final Guadalcanal night action, and the US also loses two admirals, so hectic is the conflict.

## *** PARADISE BECKONS ***

By December 1942, after the combined Marine and Army divisions eliminate most of the Japanese troops from Guadalcanal, the battle-weary malaria-infested First Marine Division is officially relieved by the Americal Division and shipped to Australia for well-deserved R&R (rest and recuperation). At first they are taken to a swampy area near tropical Brisbane, up north near the equator, but after complaining vigorously they are welcomed by the City of Melbourne with its cooler and drier southeast climate, which feels like paradise to the emaciated and diseased Marines.

The City of Melbourne billets them in the Melbourne Cricket Ground, which previously housed a US Army Air Corps unit. Several award ceremonies are held there, accompanied by stirring martial music by a resurrected Marine Band. Among the several Medal of Honor and Navy Cross awards are promotions for officers and men. Billy Bridgewater becomes a sergeant and is assigned to a platoon in Baker Company, and both Jones twins are made corporals to help train the thousands of new Marine replacements that will be arriving from the new Camp Pendleton in the spring of '43.

Many wounded or sick Marines are hospitalized at a special wing of Melbourne's municipal hospital. Alex Jones, who was shot in the right thigh, is among the invalids. Ajax is able to visit his twin brother once a week as Christmas 1942 approaches, and on one of those visits he excitedly announces that he is engaged to be married—to an Australian girl!

"Bro, this is the happiest week of my life. Mary Ellen Thomas is the most wonderful young lady in the whole universe, I swear. Her parents are great as well. They have a son in the Aussie Army, fighting in North Africa, and they make me feel like I am their son too."

"Well that's great, Ajax, but has the colonel agreed to sign your papers? You can't get married without that little piece of paper, y'know."

"Sure I know that and yes, he has agreed. Some other guys are asking for permission too, and I guess it depends on the bride's parents giving permission as well. So, will you be our Best Man if you're not too gimpy after the operation?"

"Why hell yes, you know that. So when is the big date? I won't be out of here until mid-January, probably. How did you meet Miss Mary Ellen anyway, and how will you support her on a corporal's pay and allowances?"

"No worry, Bro. When the damned war is over I'll get out of the Corps and move here to Oz to work for Mary Ellen's dad. He owns a shipyard!"

# CHAPTER FOUR

*** *TURNING THE TIDE* ***

*PT Boat Crews at "Calvertville" on Tulagi*

## *** THE PT BOATS ARRIVE ***

In October 1942, a handful of Navy people arrive on Tulagi to begin surveying the island for a suitable location to operate a PT Boat base. The boats have been operating and training at an island called Taboga near the Pacific Ocean side of the Panama Canal, with the responsibility of defending that important waterway against potential enemy attacks or sabotage. A couple of the Panama PT squadrons will soon be sent to Tulagi from Noumea, where they were delivered by cargo ships a few weeks before.

Frustrated by the almost nightly reinforcement of Japanese troops and supplies on Guadalcanal, General Vandegrift appeals through Navy channels for some sort of nighttime sea patrol to intercept the clandestine Japanese landings at each end of the big island. An Australian Coastwatcher Martin Clemens and his native crew keep the Marines fully informed of Japanese activities that they can observe from their hideouts in the mountainous interior of Guadalcanal, but the Marines themselves are unable to intercept those nighttime enemy landings..

One of the bravest and most fearless of the natives, a ferocious-looking fellow named Vouza, is awarded the Silver Star medal by General Vandegrift and is made an honorary Sergeant Major in the US Marines. Vouza was captured and tortured by the Japanese and left for dead, but he managed to chew through his bindings and crawl to the American lines, where he was received and sheltered with great accolades.

After some deliberations, the Navy's solution to night interceptions is to establish a base on Tulagi for several squadrons of Patrol Torpedo Boats that had been inspired by British designs in the European Theater. PT Boats had assisted admirably with the defense of Pearl Harbor, so a certain Navy lieutenant commander is sent to Guadalcanal/Tulagi to check things out.

Bongo Perkins arrives at Tulagi on a PBY Catalina from Fiji, where he travelled to the previous day from Sydney on a C47. His flights were uneventful, since Japan had never managed to execute its plan to capture British Fiji, French New Caledonia, and the British-French New Hebrides islands.

Bongo is met by Lt. Commander Allen Calvert USN, who has only just arrived on Tulagi himself and is due to take command of the PT Boat squadrons once the future base becomes operational. Half a dozen boats of RON-5 in Panama—PT-109 through 114—were already delivered to Noumea by commercial freighter, so there is an urgency to get a plan in place for the Tulagi base. Those boats—soon to be supplemented by the rest of RON-5 with PTs 103 through 108—are the first of a new 80-foot design from ELCO, the Electric Boat Company of New Jersey. The 12-boat series is known as the PT-103 Class. Their extra length and buoyancy enables them to carry heavier weaponry for offensive tactics such as intercepting the Japanese barges at night that are delivering troops and supplies to Guadalcanal.

"So what are your ideas, Allen," Bongo asks of his equal-rank host as they share a drink under a Tulagi palm tree.

"I'm not yet sure what to suggest, Bongo, but I can tell you that the former Jap seaplane base on Tanambogo will definitely not be suitable. It has way too small a turning basin for these new ELCOs, and there's no room to build a drydock or machine shop. Let's look at this end of Tulagi in the morning. Another Gimlet?"

Bongo welcomes the refreshing gin drink that he has only once encountered before.

"Yes indeed. Say, what are these great drinks made from, besides gin?"

"Well, you pour some gin over ice, then add the secret ingredient, which is sweet-tasting Rose's Lime Juice, and stir the mixture with vigor," his companion replies, illustrating each step. "Voila!" he adds, handing Bongo a fresh drink.

"Yeah, but what if I can't find any Rose's Lime Juice or any vigor?" Bongo smiles.

"Ha. Then you're out of luck, and you'll have to be satisfied with a Singapore Sling, which uses regular lime juice and less vigor," is the reply.

"So where did you learn about these British concoctions, Allen? I understand that you've only been here a day longer than me. I knew a Brit named Perry in Hawaii, but he never revealed any of these trade secrets to me."

"Well, you're perhaps not seagoing Navy, eh Bongo? I was a destroyer man until two weeks ago, and we met up with British and Aussie ships all over the Pacific before the war started. After a few parties their secrets were out, y'see. Cheers."

The following morning a fairly good solution is found for the new PT Boat facility after half a dozen sailors lead the way through a muddy patch of jungle on Tulagi's north shore, to a calm little bay that fronts onto Florida Island. Its local name was Sesapi Cove, where some Navy fishing enthusiasts had gone now and then. The trail started out past some former native huts that were presently used for officers' quarters, but the explorers see that the muddy ground will have to be tamed somehow, to prevent muck from getting tracked into the boats.

"Not to worry, Bongo, we can surely get a donation of Marsden matting from the Seabees over there on the Canal who are working on the airfield. That should help with the muddy parts of the trail. Otherwise, how does that little cove look to you?"

"Well fine, I guess," Bongo replies. "You know, I'm not really a PT guy. I'm only here because my ex-boss Admiral Brady at Pearl was also in charge of the PT flotilla there, and I guess that association got into my personnel records, or else he volunteered me in the hope that some PT knowhow might have rubbed off from those Pearl Harbor days. It's funny how the Navy works sometimes."

"Beautiful example I should say, but what is your field of expertise if it isn't PT Boats?"

"Oh, nothing special," Bongo says, "I'm just a general-purpose helper from time to time, you know, somebody on call for jobs no one else wants."

"Hmm, that's pretty evasive. Sounds like the ONI if you ask me."

"Oh, good grief no," Bongo throws up his hands. "You have to be really sharp to get into that outfit. By the way—not to change the subject—but when will you be back here to take over the flotilla?"

*PT Boat delivery to Tulagi*

"Not for a couple of months, unfortunately. I have to go to the PT School at Melville Rhode Island for familiarization with the boats, and then take a month's leave. My wife has been after me for ages about the latter, and I've got three and a half months accrued. Anyway, I'm so glad to have the chance to help pick out Sesapi Cove for the boats when they get here, and to meet you, Bongo. Maybe you can get back here next year to see it operational. It's funny that neither of us was trained at Melville yet here we are scoping out a new PT Boat base and even a floating drydock. What'll they think of next, eh?"

Six months later when Bongo sends his Sydney assistant Lt.(j.g.) Robert McGowan USN to inspect the new PT base on Tulagi, the amphibious PBY that brings McGowan to Henderson Field is jumped by a Japanese Zero just as it is landing. The PBY flips over and catches fire, but one of the blister gunners manages to pull himself and McGowan free of the inferno. All others aboard are killed in the crash, and the Zero gets away in spite of Henderson's antiaircraft guns. Bongo relays the sad news to Peter Perry in Sydney the next time they get together for the occasional beer. Perry is by that time a part-time undercover civilian volunteer with the ONI, in spite of being a British subject.

In due course, the PT Boats are deployed in The Slot (an alternative name for Iron Bottom Sound) on a nightly basis to intercept Japanese barges that attempt to land reinforcements on Guadalcanal, often accompanied by high-speed destroyers seeking to torpedo the PTs, which in turn are seeking to torpedo the destroyers. Each night is a time of high tension and occasional high drama, but eventually Guadalcanal is freed of enemy troops and the PT base is moved further along The Slot in the direction of Bougainville, a new objective for US strategists.

Peter Perry, who completed his engineering contract for Canton Island and his subsequent transmittal of secret information from there to the US Navy in Hawaii, is on the verge of leaving Sydney for a new job in Nouméa, New Caledonia, when Bongo drops by to discuss the recent Battle of Midway that was such a devastating setback for Japan. Peter has heard about Midway, but not to the full extent that Bongo reveals, concerning the code breakers' role in the dramatic US victory.

"I think we're on a roll at last, Peter. Nouméa probably won't be a critical base for much longer, would be my guess. The Froggies will probably be glad to be rid of us. I guess you know that New Caledonia was once a French penal colony, and many of the former internees were given land to help populate the island."

"No, I didn't know that, "Peter replies, "but that fact is probably irrelevant now, just as the British once having a penal colony here in Australia is irrelevant."

"You may think so, Peter old chap, but many people feel that both cases are definitely still relevant, including the former Brit penal colony in the state of Georgia USA. After the war those will be hot topics again, I imagine. Anyway, no point arguing. I wanted to let you know that I'll be in Nouméa in a few weeks and will look you up over there. I hope the French food is still good."

## *** NEW CALEDONIA ***

As he promised to Peter Perry a few weeks earlier, Bongo Perkins does arrive in Nouméa, the capital of New Caledonia, but for a different reason than originally planned, which was to interview a prospective ONI candidate who was working with the Navy detachment at the Nouméa seaplane base. Instead, Bongo's visit from Sydney Australia this time is to investigate rumors that New Caledonia might be likely to change its alliance from the Free French to the Vichy French regime that is under Nazi German control. If that rumor has any substance, it could create serious difficulties for the American presence on the island.

Although the Army's Americal Division had long ago departed from New Caldonia for Guadalcanal to earn its place in history, there was still a small US Marine detachment on the island, preparing to train a company of M4 Sherman tanks for future use in the Pacific. The tanks had recently been delivered from Jacques Farm Marine Base in California, but the tank crews had not yet arrived in Nouméa.

Bongo's friend and ONI collaborator Peter Perry was involved in New Caledonia with the Marine tanks as a civilian contractor, to develop wooden bridge designs that could support the 30-ton weight of those tanks on various Pacific islands.

Bongo has his taxi driver toot the car's horn as Peter emerges from his hotel early in the morning. Peter approaches the taxi and peers inside.

"Oh it's you at last! Very good, I was wondering when you would pay a visit to this delightful island paradise." Peter shakes hands with Bongo through the car window.

"Aye, it is indeed me, Peter. I need some help with an investigation for our benevolent lord and master, Uncle Sam. Can we go somewhere for a cup of coffee?"

"Why certainly," Peter replies, climbing into the back seat with Bongo. "I was just going to the Marine camp to check some dimensions, but that can wait. Shall I suggest a spot for the coffee and a bite of breakfast?"

"Please do," Bongo answers, "and tell the driver for me. He and I can't communicate. I had to show him a piece of paper with the name of your hotel."

When they are comfortably settled at *Chez Louise*, Peter's favorite Noumea restaurant, Bongo fills Peter in about the disturbing rumor that has been circulating in Australia.

"Absolute rubbish!" Peter exclaims. "We have heard that rumor over here as well, and the people are very upset about it. I'm told that the governor will make an official announcement to that effect in a few days."

"So New Caledonia is still solidly with General Charles de Gaulle and the Free French then? Is that what you're saying?"

"Absolutely!" Peter emphasizes. "I have several local acquaintances now, you know, and this matter is discussed every time I see them. There is no need to worry about that, Bongo, but whoever started the rumor ought to be horsewhipped!"

"I fully agree; if only we could find out who that person is. By the way, Peter, before I return to Sydney, would you like to show me what you are working on with the Marines?"

"Mmm, perhaps. It's not just the Marine tankers who are coming here to this island; there is also a headquarters group for some larger unit somewhere in the Pacific. I've noticed lots of high-ranking officers coming and going, including some admirals and generals. I'd love for you to come and see my first wooden tank bridge—I mean my first wooden bridge for steel tanks—but I have a special permit to come and go from the base, whereas you ... "

"Hey, silly Brit, I'm authorized to go anywhere that the US has facilities. Let's grab another taxi and go see this wooden masterpiece of yours."

When the taxi drops them off at the Marine base, the gate guard waves Peter through, whom he recognizes, but then salutes Bongo and asks for his ID. After reviewing it, the guard salutes Bongo again and picks up a phone to order a vehicle "for a naval officer and a civilian."

"That's a treat," Peter says to Bongo. "I usually have to walk from here to the warehouse over there where the tanks are kept," pointing at a building some 200 yards away..

A few minutes later, a green staff car arrives and its driver opens the rear doors for the two visitors, saluting Bongo as they climb aboard. After Peter asks the driver to take them to the tank building, the driver turns and tells them "Sorry sir, the colonel is waiting to pay his respects," and promptly drives them away in a different direction.

"Hmm," Bongo mutters.

"Mmm," Peter echoes.

After some 15 minutes the car pulls up at a large green tent that is part of a collection of them in neat rows behind a long hedge. In the grass outside the large tent is a red sign with yellow letters:

**Headquarters Commanding General**
**First Marine Amphibious Corps**

A neatly uniformed Marine lieutenant colonel in dungarees introduces himself and exchanges salutes with Bongo, after smiling and shaking hands with Peter:

"Merrill Twining, Gentlemen. C3 Operations for IMAC." After querying Bongo about his naval background, Colonel Twining asks Peter whether he has heard about the change in plans for the tank company. Peter shakes his head, feeling both curious and somewhat concerned.

"Mr Perry, I'm afraid the tank crews will not be coming to Nouméa after all. Some of those tanks will be shipped to Guadalcanal very soon for jungle training, and others will be stored here for future destinations. Your excellent wooden bridge will remain in New Caledonia for posterity and will be put to good use as our IMAC organization builds up for another assignment in this lengthy war. I hope you are not too disappointed, sir."

Turning to Bongo, he continues: "May I offer you gentlemen a special treat from the European Theater? Some fine Irish whiskey, for example?" Bongo replies affirmatively for both of them while Peter's mind is racing. *I must find the Contracts Office director at once! What will happen to me now that this project has been cancelled.?* He barely hears Bongo and the Marine officer clinking their glasses.

*P38 Lightnings moving carefully through Noumea from harbor to an airfield*

# CHAPTER FIVE

## *** THE CARTWHEELS ***

*War-Stressed PT Boats in New Guinea with torpedoes no longer launched from tubes.*

In the spring of 1943, the Allied campaign to defeat Japan became a two-pronged attack that was developed with MacArthur's Army and Nimitz's Navy being like two cartwheel tracks aimed at isolating Japan's major base at Rabaul to the north of New Guinea. While the Solomon Islands were being neutralized and Guadalcanal was becoming a rear echelon staging base with four airfields capable of bomber or fighter use, MacArthur began to focus on clearing Japanese troops from the huge island of New Guinea, while asking help from Nimitz with the Rabaul strategy.

This was where Allied policy changed from direct invasion to forced isolation of Japanese strongpoints. Because of the lengthy time it had been taking to clear the Solomons, and in view of the high casualties that had been inflicted on the Marines, Army, and Navy, it became more sensible to just isolate and bypass Japanese strongpoints wherever practical, and by means of daily air surveillance and attacks, to keep their garrisons from escaping. This was to be the new Allied strategy for dealing with Japan's heavily fortified base at Rabaul, which the cartwheels would drive into isolation.

## *** NEW GEORGIA IN THE SOLOMONS ***

After finally ridding Guadalcanal of Japanese troops by February 1943, with the great assistance of PT Boats operating at night from Sesapi Cove on Tulagi, US forces began a northwest push along the Solomon Island chain in the direction of Bougainville where the Japanese were still strongly entrenched. Defeating Japan in the Solomons would open the door to neutralizing their heavily defended base at Rabaul. It would also open a way towards the Marianas from where bombers could reach Japan on a daily basis.

After their loss of Guadalcanal and Tulagi, the next Japanese defensive point in the Solomons was a complex group of islands known as New Georgia, located about halfway between Guadalcanal and Bougainville. In anticipation of a lengthy New Georgia conflict, the PT boats were first moved from Tulagi to the Russells, a relatively peaceful pair of mosquito-free islands—Pavuvu and Banika—to prepare a rear echelon base that will be closer to the next battle zone.

Pavuvu gets assigned to the First Marine Division as a future recuperation and training locale, whose stark contrast with Melbourne makes Marine veterans hate the place. By contrast, the PT people come to love nearby Banika for its stress-free ambience where they can get an adult drink and shoot the breeze while their boats get slowly refilled with high octane aviation gasoline from 50-gallon drums, a thankless task for junior crew members and shore-based support personnel. In April while the PT Boats are getting organized at Banika, a controversial event takes place far down The Slot near the large island of Bougainville, which is still very much under Japanese control.

The controversial event is the death of Admiral Yamamoto, the highest-ranking admiral in the IJN. The admiral's plane and its escorts get intercepted by an Army Air Corps squadron of long-range P-38 "Lightning" fighter planes from Guadalcanal, after codebreakers intercept a message stating that Admiral Yamamoto will be making an inspection tour of Bougainville on such-and-such a date, leaving from Rabaul at a specific time.

The well-planned interception becomes controversial because it is viewed by some as a leadership assassination, since the Japanese plane was essentially ambushed based on foreknowledge; but to many others the deed is hailed as timely revenge for the Pearl Harbor attack that Yamamoto himself meticulously planned and executed. The intercept was approved by Admiral Nimitz and delegated to Admiral Halsey's organization, which in turn selected the Army P-38's long-range capability for a flight that takes them over 1100 miles there and back.

The plan is totally successful; Admiral Yamamoto's plane crashes into the jungle at the east end of Bougainville, and all the P-38s return safely to Guadalcanal. When Japanese searchers locate the plane wreck, they find the admiral's body thrown out from the crash, still strapped to his seat and clutching his ceremonial sword.

In June 1943, the New Georgia campaign begins with weeks of extensive bombardment of a Japanese airfield at Munda Point, that they had tried to hide by tying coconut branches to wires stretched across the runway. The PTs move their base from the Russells to Rendova, an island closer to the battle zone. There are nineteen boats at this point, which patrol the wide waterways at night, searching for enemy ships or barges. A few of the PTs have radar by then, so those are used as lead boats for groups of three or four. Many of the boats no longer operate within their original squadrons but get allocated to various smaller nighttime groups according to their armaments or their tactical experience.

On one particular night, the Rendova base gets alerted to a fleet of four Japanese destroyers bringing supplies and reinforcements to New Georgia, so Rendova musters its fifteen serviceable boats to search for targets.

"Hey Jack," Richard Keresey, the skipper of PT-105 shouts to John F. Kennedy, his counterpart on PT-109, as they tromp down to the boats as darkness begins to fall. "Good hunting tonight. Watch out for the reefs in Blackett Strait."

"Yeah, thanks Gunga, same to you and your guys. Last one back is a rotten egg!"

Skippers Joe Roberts of PT-103 and Dave Payne of PT-106 also heed Keresey's advice, but unfortunately Kennedy becomes the rotten egg when his 109 boat is run down and cut in half by a speeding Japanese destroyer in the dark of that night, an event that doubtless startles both parties. Two of the 109 boat's crew are lost when fuel tanks explode and the stern section sinks from the weight of its three Packard engines. The 109's bow section stays afloat, however, and the eleven survivors huddle in it until dawn.

Kennedy and the others eventually make it back to Rendova, emaciated from swimming four miles from the wrecked boat to a remote islet and then thrashing their way through jungle foliage for several days in search of help, living off coconuts until coastwatchers find them and summon a PT Boat to retrieve them.

Finally in November the New Georgia landings begin. A feint landing on the nearby large island of Choiseul is led by Lt. Colonel Victor Krulak USMC, although one of its columns has to be rescued by a couple of Rendova-based PTs, including a boat skippered by Jack Kennedy *[future US President–Ed.]*, just recovered from his PT-109 ordeal and seeking further adventures.

The main landings on New Georgia eventually succeed in capturing the airfield at Munda, its main objective, thereby ending the four-month campaign. The way is finally clear for assaulting the much larger island of Bougainville.

## *** BOUGAINVILLE IN THE SOLOMONS ***

The Bougainville campaign begins with a successful landing of some 30,000 US Marine and Army troops at Torokina Bay, accompanied once again with a diversionary landing by a Marine platoon on Choiseul. In a flashback to Guadalcanal, General Vandegrift leads the Marines ashore, although this time it is the Third Marine Division together with the

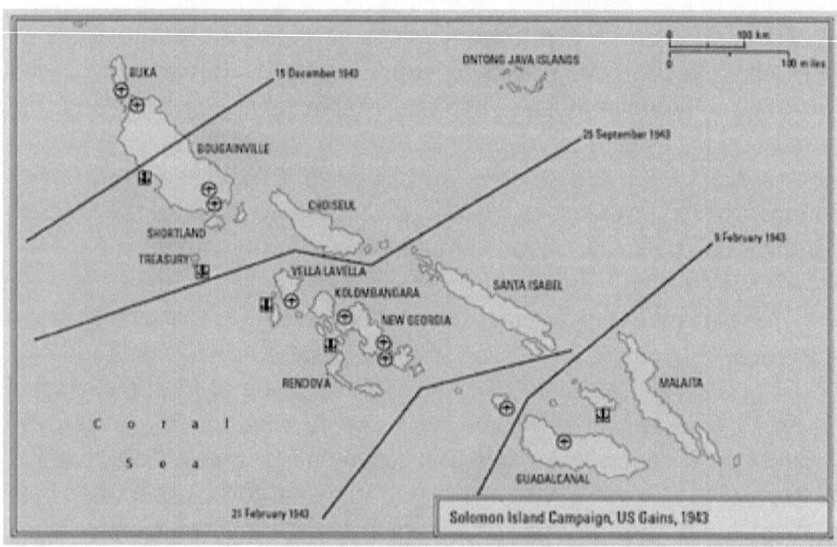

Army's Americal companions. In the map above, the reader can see the approximate timescale for the overall Solomon Island campaigns that began in August 1942 at Guadalcanal. The eventual Allied air bases are also shown on this map.

Bougainville is another long campaign that begins in November 1943 and lasts until late 1944 when Australian troops relieve the weary Marines. The Australians continue their mop-up until August 1945 when the Pacific War ends, but many other battles take place during the same period. Allied airfields that are quickly constructed within range of Rabaul are greatly facilitated by aerial photos from VMD-254 (Marine) and VD-1 (Navy) photographic squadrons flying B-24s from Guadalcanal and from Piva on Bougainville, even though Japanese troops are still present in other parts of Bougainville. Until the Pacific War ends in August 1945, Rabaul will be overflown on a daily basis to ensure no reinforcements are being delivered or soldiers evacuated.

Soon after the Bougainville campaign begins, MacArthur "borrows" the First Marine Division—still enjoying the pleasures of Melbourne— to make a landing on New Britain's Cape Gloucester as Allied planes from Bougainville attack Rabaul in a pincer movement to try destroying Japanese planes as a prelude to isolating its garrison of 40,000 troops. The dense and malaria-ridden jungles of Cape Gloucester are a hard slog for troops of the Old Breed, who afterwards are taken to Pavuvu in the Russells for recuperation. Melbourne is just a dream by then.

"OK Bro, see you on the beach," yells Ajax to his brother Alex after 1/5 is loaded at Goodenough Island into LTV Amtracs, to become the first wave ashore on the east side of New Britain's Cape Gloucester on 26 December 1943. Christmas Day is spent packing up and checking equipment, with a little extra chow to mark the theoretical holiday (that also marks exactly two years since the Japanese capture of British Hong Kong – Ed.).

As the target island is reached a few hours later, and as LTVs and the occasional M4 Sherman tank roll into the choppy surf from the maws of large LSTs, Alex waves back a quick thumbs-up then ducks as flashes of light among the trees behind the beach indicate the presence of enemy defenders firing at them. Occasional pings on the metal sides of the Amtracs confirm the threat that the boatloads will face.

The parallel lines of Amtracs roll and toss in the windy surf, but become steadier as their bows and tracks finally bite into the sand and the clanking vehicles churn slowly up the beach toward the tree line where those deadly lights still twinkle, leaving behind a series of wavy tracks in the sand as if gigantic tortoises are frolicking after a morning dip in the ocean.

Two Navy gunners in each LTV keep up steady bursts from their twin 50-caliber machine guns that shred the leaves of the nearest trees, hoping to knock out the Japanese soldiers who are targeting their Marines as they roll over the sides of the LTVs and dive prone onto the sand.

"Keep moving, you people!" yells platoon sergeant Billy Bridgewater to the clusters of new Marine recruits that had joined the battalion in Australia. "You wanna stay here and get your asses shot off? Get going, head for those trees and kill the bastards who are firing at us! Move it; move it!"

Urged on by the Jones brothers and other squad leaders, and further emboldened by 75mm blasts from the M4 tanks, the Marines rise as a line abreast and charge the trees, firing and yelling as they swoop into the jungle, searching for fresh meat. It is soon over, as there are no real fortifications on that beachline, and the entire east coast is not heavily defended. 1/5 is only there to make a decoy landing and draw Japanese troops away from the west side of Cape Gloucester, where the main Allied force will soon be landing, led by Major General William Rupertus who was Vandegrift's assistant commander back on Guadalcanal. The task of 1/5 now is to fight its way through the dense jungle to join up with the rest of the first Marine Division on the other side of the cape.

Easier said than done! The real enemy for all combatants on Cape Gloucester becomes the soggy rotting jungle itself. It is still 26 December 1943, and the battle for Cape Gloucester will not be over for three more weeks. Several hundred Marines will be dead by then, with many more wounded, but the mission will eventually be accomplished and the noose will be that much tighter around the Japanese stronghold on Rabaul.

"What an asshole place that was," says Alex Jones while sipping a cold beer with Billy Bridgewater and Ajax at the NCO tent on Pavuvu, the day after the Marines are brought back from Cape Gloucester. "I hope we never have to see jungle again—never!" The trio drink solemnly to that pledge, knowing however that that fate is a fickle mistress.

By February 1944, when Rabaul has been fully isolated, MacArthur's troops in New Guinea begin moving by ship along its northern coast, attacking every fourth or fifth Japanese coastal stronghold and isolating the others. PT Boats are used for attacking Japanese shipping that attempts to evacuate the bypassed bases. The veteran PT-105 is among the newly formed RON 18 on New Guinea which is given that cleanup assignment.

## *** TERRIBLE TARAWA ***

Two months earlier, while the Nimitz Cartwheel was converging on Bougainville to destroy its aviation assets in November 1943, the Second Marine Division was ordered to attack a small island called Betio in the Tarawa Atoll of the British Gilbert Islands *(today's Kiribati – Ed.)*.

Of comparable size to Tulagi, tiny Betio (pronounced "Besho") is roughly 2.5 x 0.8 miles in area. In 1943 it included a closely guarded Japanese airfield defended by hundreds of concrete pillboxes and heavy artillery, manned by nearly 5,000 Japanese troops and Korean laborers. Onto this small island the Marines landed around 11,000 men over a protective reef and through a lagoon, to capture the island's strategic airfield.

Even though former British residents had warned Navy planners about seasonal neap tides that would affect the ability of small boats to cross Betio's reef, the neutralization of its airfield was thought to be a critical obstacle to enabling future westward attacks on the Marshall Islands and the Marianas. It was only in early 1944 that the US strategy evolved into bypassing and blockading heavily fortified islands like Betio (e.g. Rabaul).

The Betio attack went ahead on the assumption that there would be five feet of water over the reef at high tide, whereas the reality was just four feet due to the neap tide, as the British had warned. Although the leading wave of Marines travelling in LVT amphibious vehicles with tractor treads did manage the reef crossing, the majority of the remaining troops and light vehicles were loaded into Higgins Boats which could not cross. This problem caused most of the Marines having to disembark in full view of Japanese shore guns, while they either tried to haul their empty boats across the reef or else tried to wade the chest-high lagoon for several hundred yards, under intense enemy fire in both cases.

Casualties began to mount alarmingly, with dead Marines floating in the lagoon or collapsing on the sandy beach if they made it that far. Once the surviving Marines got away from the beach they were faced with disabling hundreds of pillboxes and bunkers one by one, using flamethrowers and grenades. The putrid stench of death was everywhere as the intense battle raged onwards and casualties mounted on both sides.

*Marines stuck on a Tarawa reef in their Higgins Boat*

The Tarawa campaign saw the Marines' first use of M4 (Sherman) medium tanks in combat. Fourteen M4s accompanied the invasion force and were unloaded at the reef to make their way ashore through the theoretically shallow lagoon, but due to large underwater craters caused by US naval gunfire—into which half a dozen of the tanks disappeared from sight—or from Japanese mines in the lagoon or their shore-based artillery, only two of the fourteen tanks actually made it ashore in one piece! Those two became highly valued for their 75mm guns which destroyed many enemy pillboxes.

A disabled tank can be seen in the following photo with its five-man crew awaiting a tow. The beach is still littered with dead Marine infantry after the fighting ended.

AUSTRALIAN WAR MEMORIAL                                    PO2018.252

The gruesome battle for Betio lasted 76 non-stop hours, during which there were more dead and wounded Marines than the entire six months of the Guadalcanal campaign! The Empire of Japan was certainly a formidable adversary!

Ironically, another island in the Tarawa atoll called Makin, that had been assigned to the Army, was scarcely militarized at all. It contained a Japanese seaplane base with just a few hundred defenders. Makin was seized in less than a day, a stark contrast to Betio with its neap tide problem and its heavily guarded airfield.

# CHAPTER SIX

## *** NEW GUINEA AND THE MARIANAS ***

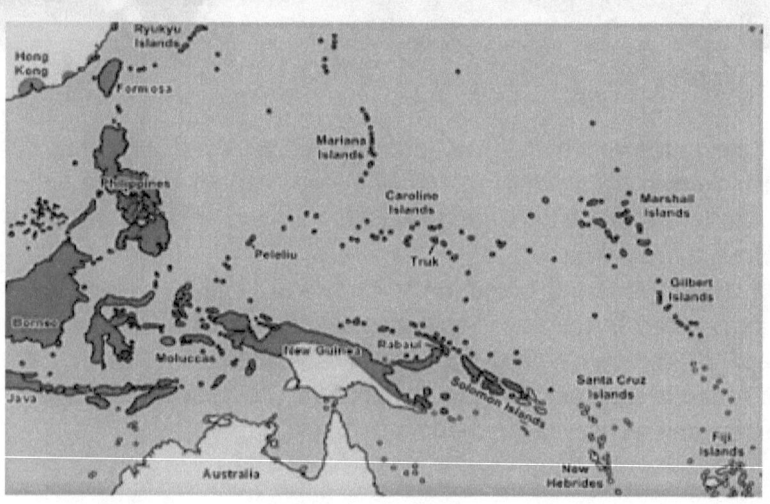

*The Pacific War in 1944 - light color Allies; dark color Japan*

MacArthur's cartwheel continues along the north coast of New Guinea, bypassing or pushing the Japanese inland to where the Australians can deal with them, as they already did by blocking Port Moresby from a Japanese attack along the Kokoda Trail..

After Australia gives the Allies a good start on the north coast of New Guinea, the port of Hollandia becomes a key Allied harbor and staging area, and it is there that several USO troupes will arrive towards the end of 1944 to entertain the troops.

Meanwhile, once Tarawa and the Gilbert Islands are secured, Nimitz's Navy and Marine forces proceed to neutralize the Marshall Islands by capturing Majuro, Kwajalein; and Eniwetok, and the Carolines with its large Truk atoll whose fleet anchorage was known to the Allies as "Japan's Pearl Harbor." Airfields in the Marshalls get quickly built in preparation for recapturing Guam and other islands of the Marianas. The Marianas will put the Japanese home islands within range of newly developed B-29 bombers, which can in turn hasten the end of the war.

Of the thirteen Mariana Islands, all except Guam had been Japanese colonies for twenty-five years and the Japanese economy was well integrated. In addition to native Chamorros, Japan brought farmers from Formosa (Taiwan) and slave laborers from Korea to try developing new crops. A rudimentary Japanese dialect became the common language of all three cultures.

Saipan, with its capital of Garapan being the administrative center for the complete Japanese Marianas chain, had a civilian population of 30,000. Korean and Formosan troops were among the IJA division that was in charge of Saipan's defense, with another 32,000 hungry mouths to feed. When that large mountainous island of 45 square miles island was selected by the Allies as its first Mariana target, the Allies hoped that Japan would expect the Marianas attack to commence with the island of Guam, the US colony that Japan had captured just a few years before.

However, in spite of a catastrophic accident in Pearl Harbor where a dozen LSTs caught fire while being loaded with munitions and fuel to support the Saipan invasion, a massive US fleet of some 500 ships—including seven fleet carriers and a dozen battleships—brought the Second and Fourth Marine Divisions and the Army's 27th Division to the Saipan landing beaches on 15 June 1944, just a day later than originally planned. It was an invasion force of some 37,000 men with around fifty Sherman tanks.

Trained at Montford Point, North Carolina, some 800 African-American Marines would unload material on the beach under enemy fire, the first Blacks to see combat in the Pacific. All the services were segregated in WWII, but overall respect for the willingness and abilities of the Blacks would bring about desegregation soon after the war ended.

Even with the numerical superiority of the Americans, the Japanese defenders on Saipan gave a good account of themselves with nighttime counterattacks and daylight defenses in volcanic caves, but after three weeks of heavy fighting when they realized all was lost, the Japanese residue launched a ferocious but futile *Banzai* attack during which almost all of them were killed. A surviving handful withdrew into the mountains with a group of civilians, and did not surrender until November 1945, three months after the Pacific War officially ended.

When the main Japanese force was defeated, Japanese civilians led a thousand or more local men and women to commit suicide by jumping from high cliffs into the sea, claiming that they would be tortured by the American invaders. Marpi Point is still memorialized today because of that senseless tragedy.

During the early part of the land battle for Saipan, Japan decided to attack the US fleet over several days with both carrier planes and land based aircraft from the Philippines, thinking to cripple its Allied adversary. However, many of the Japanese pilots were inadequately trained, with the resulting loss of 600 Japanese planes and three aircraft carriers. The battle was so one-sided that US pilots referred to this Battle of the Philippine Sea as the "Marianas Turkey Shoot." The US by contrast lost 130 planes, mostly from crack-ups on carrier landings or from running out of fuel.

On the Japanese home front, Prime Minister Tojo who was one of the more vocal sponsors of the war, resigned his post after Saipan was lost. He was later hung by the Allies as a war criminal.

The next phase of the Mariana campaign was the recovery of Guam, and with it a clever capture of Tinian. The original date for recapturing Guam was June 18th, 1944, but because of the Battle of the Philippine Sea and the tenacity of Japan's Saipan defenders, it was postponed until July 21st. Unfortunately, however, the preinvasion naval bombardment of Guam proceeded according to both the original June plan and the rescheduled July invasion, with the result that Guam and its capital Agaña were pounded to rubble unnecessarily for many weeks.

On the following page, the top photo shows the Agaña fairgrounds a decade before the Pacific War began, and the bottom one shows Agaña after the multiple US bombardments.

At any rate, led by Major General Roy Geiger USMC, the Guam invasion finally took place with five Marine battalions— the Third Marine Division plus a reinforced brigade—attacking beaches at the north and south coasts. Marines were met by zealous Japanese defenders who had survived the month-long US bombardments.

Many of the Guam invasion elements came down from Saipan even before the latter was completely secured. A long Allied flotilla was anxiously watched by Japanese forces on Tinian as the Allied transports and warships steamed on by toward Guam. Tinian is just a few miles south of Saipan, whereas Guam is over a hundred miles farther south. By the third morning, the last of the Allied forces for Guam appeared to be ending, when suddenly a group of ships at the tail end of that convoy abruptly peeled off and delivered a detachment of Marines to the south

end of Tinian. Caught off guard, the Japanese response to this feint was slow but steady, and it was only realized a few hours later that a main US force had been landed on Tinian's northern beaches.

By the time another Japanese response got organized, enough of the main US force was ashore to defend itself. Heavy artillery from Saipan was also brought to bear against the Japanese, and Tinian was declared secure after only 10 days. Work immediately took place to extend the Japanese airfields so that B-29's could land and take off. Saipan and particularly Tinian were quickly developed into robust air bases for the bombing of Japan's home islands.

Meanwhile, Guam was better defended than Tinian, and the fighting went into the first week of August, after which Guam was developed into a major Allied logistical base to support the forthcoming invasion of the Philippines.

While the Marianas were being secured by Nimitz's Navy and Marines, MacArthur's Army was pushing its way westward along the New Guinea coast with the help of PT Boats and destroyers.

New Guinea is the world's second largest island with an area of 380,000 square miles and a 1,600 mile northern coast. So effective were the US Army's efforts at cleaning out the Japanese resistance along that lengthy north coast, that the USO was given approval in late 1944 to start bringing its Camp Shows to Hollandia in New Guinea. By the time the USO got this organized it was early 1945.

## *** TROUPES FOR THE TROOPS ***

Most of the earlier USO performers were singles or small acts like Bob Hope and his friends (below) who performed at rear echelon places like Nouméa earlier in the war, but later the USO began sending entire theatrical acts like *Mexican Hayride* as the Allied war buildup grew larger.

Its shows for New Guinea become known officially as the Foxhole Circuit. Betsy (Seligmann) Berkley is among the USO dancers who sail to

Hollandia in January 1945 aboard SS *Monterey*, a former Matson Line passenger ship that was chartered by the US Maritime Commission as a fast troop ship. Designed in 1931 to carry 500 first-class passengers in prewar comfort to destinations around the Pacific Ocean, the ship had already made several trips for the Army to Hawaii and Australia.

In a letter to her mother, Betsy recalls her trip from San Francisco to New Guinea as having some 5,000 on board, a mixture of US and Canadian military, and several USO troupes including her *Mexican Hayride* entourage.

"Our stateroom was designed for two, but there were twenty girls crammed into it." she wrote, "And after we crossed the equator (and I got a shellback certificate), it got really, really hot and humid. We were issued with woolen uniforms in New York because the USO originally planned for us to go to Europe, but somehow they changed the plan but not our uniforms. We wore those darned things all along New Guinea—Hollandia, Biak, Noemfoor—until they nearly fell apart. Then we were issued army nurse uniforms which were way more comfortable."

In another letter to her mother, Betsy wrote: "In New Guinea we go from base to base as the huge island gets secured, and then they move us to Morotai in the Halmaheras. It is there that I get the surprise of my life! As usual, we did the *Mexican Hayride* routine, which by then we could all do in our sleep. That's me, the second from the left in the front row of the cast photo that they took back in New York.

"Well, as the show finishes in Morotai and we are taking our bows, I spot an old friend from Seguin sitting on a stool in the front row of the audience, and he is wearing a Navy uniform. Maybe you remember the guy I went to school with from kindergarten to high school, Clarence Saegert? We were both really surprised to see each other! I nearly fell off the stage and he nearly fell off the stool," she writes to her mother, Blanche.

*(Betsy Robinson, as she was later known, told us the rest of this story when interviewed seventy years later in Seguin Texas, where she had returned after a life of further travel and adventure – Ed.)*

After she changes from her costume, Betsy takes Clarence backstage to meet some of the cast and the manager, then Clarence invites Betsy to take a look at the PT Boat that he is in charge of. It is 25 March 1945.

"Betsy," says Clarence, "I was the executive officer, or XO, for this boat for six months off the New Guinea coast before I was made her skipper and promoted to lieutenant junior grade. Then they brought some of the boats over here to Morotai. I bet you went to a lot of our bases in New Guinea that the Japs had control of originally. But MacArthur's guys and the Aussies chased them away and we Navy guys shot up their ships and barges and sank a few too."

"That's right, Clarence," she acknowledges, as his jeep pulls up at the PT wharf, "We too hit every darned one of those liberated bases. Frankly we're all getting pretty tired of this old Broadway show and the many one-night stands, but I hear the Marianas and Philippines will be next for us. Cole Porter wrote lots of better songs than the ones for Mexican Hayride. He must have been sick or something when Mike Todd twisted his arm to write the score for this show. What did you think of it, by the way?"

"Well, it was OK, especially your dancing troupe, but the singing was, um … Look, here's my old wooden boat, and I sent the Exec to round up all the crew so they can meet you, Betsy."

"Wow, that's super nice of you. I see number 105 on the cabin or cockpit, or whatever you call it. Does that mean PT 105?"

"Sure does. This ancient boat started work in Panama way back in '42, then they brought her to the Pacific—the Solomons in April '43 and then New Guinea in '44, and now Morotai in the Halmaheras in '45. She has really been around, and will go on to the Philippines from here, no doubt."

"You could say the same thing about this old girl too, as a matter of fact—me! We've been on the road for almost six months, about as long as you, old buddy. When will you go back home?"

"Just one more month, Betsy, at the end of April. Probably before you if you're going to the Philippines. Heck, our guys are still fighting over there, so be careful. Damned Japs are holed up in Manila's old town and our troops are blasting the old Spanish walls apart to get them out. When MacArthur escaped from there in '42, he declared Manila an open city so it wouldn't be damaged, but the Jap admiral now refuses to do the same. They say it was a beautiful city before all this happened. Anyway, these PT squadrons will all go over there when things are quieter, but not with me aboard. I'm looking forward to seeing Texas and Evelyn again, and our new son for the first time. But come and meet the guys now. They want to take you for a ride around the bay in this old crate. I hope it doesn't sink from old age, but we'll put a lifejacket on you just in case!"

"Now Clarence, I hope you're just teasing." Clarence just chuckles then hands Betsy up to some welcoming hands.

"Gentlemen, please say hello to my pretty friend from Seguin Texas. We used to go to school together before the war. This is Miss Betsy Seligmann, oops, Miss Betsy Berkley is what she calls herself now that she's in show biz. Betsy, this is the best bunch of poker players in Uncle Sam's Navy, but they're still learning how to run a PT Boat, so you'd better hang tight onto something to keep from falling overboard while they figure out how to drive the boat smoothly."

Betsy shakes thirteen outstretched hands and smiles nervously at their jokes, still worried whether she will survive the trip. Suddenly she shrieks as the engines are started with a roar and the deck begins to vibrate.

"What's happening! Are we sinking?" she shouts, seeing that the boat is drifting away from the wharf.

"Maybe so," Clarence says, looking suitably solemn. "Hang on, Betsy, I'll go below and find out what the problem is!" But seeing her panicked face, he relents and tells her everything is OK, and then he tells his eager XO to "take her on out."

With an even louder roar, PT 105 lurches forward and the bow lifts up, giving Betsy some more palpitations as she grabs for a handhold, but she relaxes somewhat when she sees everyone smiling and laughing.

"You are a naughty boy, Clarence Saegert. I'll get even with you somehow, some day," she threatens.

With her hair streaming back in the rush of wind as the 105 boat speeds around the bay, Betsy begins to enjoy the wild ride. She can see the winking shore lights around the bay of Morotai, which somehow stabilize her even though the deck is seldom level as the boat cruises in a long arc. The twenty-minute excitement is exhilarating, and Betsy is smiling dreamily by the time they slow down to tie up at the wharf. There is another surprise waiting for her.

"Miss Betsy Berkley," Clarence announces formally once the boat is tied-to, "on behalf of your visit this evening, we the crew of the former PT-105 are pleased to announce that this here rejuvenated boat is to be known henceforth as the USS *Betsy!*"

Everyone gives three cheers, and an embarrassed Betsy is presented with an official-looking document that briefly states the boat's name change; it is signed by all fourteen of the officers and men. *(A copy of this document may be seen on a plaque entitled Small World in the courtyard of the National Museum of the Pacific War in Fredericksburg Texas, which is under the care of the Admiral Nimitz Foundation and former Marine Corps Commandant, General Michael Hagee, the museum's CEO – Ed.).*

Betsy's last show on the 1945 tour is at the end of April, after performing in Mindanao and Leyte in the Philippines. The Kaiser ship that is to take her troupe home breaks down near Ulithi, so they go ashore and do another performance while awaiting onward transportation. Finally they reach Pearl Harbor, where they are billeted at the Army's Schofield Barracks. Betsy eventually signs up for three more USO tours afterwards, which take her to the occupations of Japan and Korea, where we shall meet her again in the final chapter of this book.

### *** IWO JIMA ***

Bombing raids on Japan by long-range B29s from Tinian and Saipan begin in late November 1944 and continue until the war ends in August 1945. Initially the raids are high altitude so-called "precision" bombings beyond the range of Japanese fighter planes and anti-aircraft gunnery, but strong winds make it difficult to pinpoint industrial targets outside of the cities, hence the bombing is not really precise. The tactic is soon changed to lower altitude fire-bombing of inner city neighborhoods where small-scale manufacturing takes place among the paper and wooden homes that catch fire easily. As the frequency of the raids increases, the result is a horrific leveling of large cities and the deaths of thousands of civilians through incineration.

*Bomb Damage in Tokyo*

Bombings from the Marianas intensify as the Japanese Emperor continues refusing to end the war. Low altitude attacks mean that some B29s get damaged or lost to anti-aircraft and fighter plane defenses. Even though Japanese pilots in the home front are poorly trained and gunnery is sporadic, some B29 losses begin to occur, with the majority being damaged rather than shot down. As a result, an intermediate airfield is needed for allowing damaged bombers to crash-land or otherwise abort their flights instead of trying to reach the Marianas and likely getting lost at sea. An intermediate airfield will also provide for fighter plane escorts to accompany the bombers on the way to and from the target areas, thereby providing some defense against Japanese planes.

A suitable but heavily fortified island with two airfields in the Jima group is selected, being about halfway back to Tinian and Saipan from Japan. Expecting Iwo Jima to be very heavily defended, the Third, Fourth, and Fifth Marine Divisions—a total of 70,000 men—are ordered to capture it in late February 1945.

Easier said than done! Japanese defenders number around 21,000, but they are cleverly dug in and interconnected by eleven miles of tunnels. The Iwo Jima campaign lasts for twenty-five days rather than the two days originally planned for. Poor US intelligence and skillful Japanese preparations and defense account for the difference. In fact, it is later questioned why Iwo Jima was selected for invasion in the first place, as opposed to somewhere else. The reason is probably that Iwo Jima was closest geographically to the flight path back to the Marianas. At any rate, in the brutal battle for Iwo Jima, Marine casualties exceed those of the Japanese for the only time in the Pacific war, with nearly one third of the landing force being hors de combat (although Japanese deaths were highest). Admiral Nimitz's staff planned the Iwo Jima invasion without consulting the Marine Corps, announcing that it would be over within a couple of days.

### *** THE USO ON GUAM ***

So fast is the Allied advance moving towards Japan itself, that Agaña is nearly rebuilt and Guam is being turned into a rear echelon base by the time Betsy's next USO troupe arrives there to entertain the troops. Admiral Nimitz even moves his headquarters to Guam from Hawaii as the Pacific war enters its final phase, and Captain "Hi Yo" Silvers, who had replaced Commodore "Stoney" Wall as Bongo's ONI boss, was transferred there as well.

In addition to the *Mexican Hayride* production, some of the cast display their talents at a beach on Guam. The following photo—with Betsy Berkley at the left (on the trio's right)—became a 1945 Life Magazine centerfold.

# CHAPTER SEVEN

## *** *THE PHILIPPINES AND OKINAWA* ***

*African-American Marines on Peleliu take a break in 115-degree heat*

While the bombing of major cities in Japan continues apace, massive US fleets get organized to lead the way for the recovery of the Philippine Islands. The original Allied plan was to invade the large southern Philippine island of Mindanao. For this, a preliminary attack on Peleliu in the Japanese mandate islands of Palau was required, in order to capture its airfield and protect the eastern flank of the Mindanao invasion force.

However, a month or so before the Mindanao invasion Admiral "Bull" Halsey, noting the heavy Japanese aviation losses from "The Marianas

Turkey Shoot," recommended to Admiral Nimitz that Mindanao could be cancelled and the more northern Philippine island of Leyte could be invaded instead, which is closer to Manila, the capital on Luzon island.

General MacArthur agrees that the Peleliu campaign is no longer necessary, but Nimitz (who was in Quebec with the other Allied leaders) replies that the Peleliu invasion fleet of 1600 ships is already at sea and will be difficult to turn back just two days before the scheduled landings, and that Intelligence has indicated Peleliu will be an easy campaign *(déjà vu – Ed.)*. Nimitz therefore lets the Peleliu attack proceed "to give new replacements in the First Marine Division some useful practice," or words to that effect. It turns out to be a disastrous decision, once again based on faulty US intelligence.

## *** PELELIU ***

The Peleliu campaign that began on 15 September 1944 has the distinction of being one of the bloodiest battles fought by the United States in the Pacific Theater. Peleliu was defended by 11,000 Japanese troops who were well dug in with concrete bunkers (as in Betio) and connected by caves and underground tunnels (as in Iwo Jima) and supported by tanks (as in Saipan). Japan had 25 years to prepare for the defense of this mandated island, which could have been bypassed as Admiral Halsey suggested.

The Old Breed suffers enormous casualties in the terrible heat before the island is finally secured 73 days later. In this campaign, the First Marine Division is again led by Major General William Rupertus, who estimates a 4-day battle and keeps pushing his Marines into unnecessary danger in order to justify his prediction, which had been leaked to the press. In reserve at a less well-defended Palau island is the Army's 81st Infantry Division, known as the "Wildcats." They are soon needed.

The 5th Marine Regiment under Colonel Harold "Bucky" Harris is assigned to capture the Peleliu airfield, which they do after eleven days of hard fighting. During that part of the battle, First Sergeant Billy Bridgewater of Able Company is killed by a Japanese sniper while conferring with his company commander, and so are newly-wed Corporal Ajax Jones and a Navy corpsman who had both come to Billy's aid.

Ajax's twin brother Alex—screaming "you goddam sons-a-bitches"— is later awarded the Navy Cross for single-handedly clearing out the sniper bunker's three occupants with rifle fire and hand grenades, although he gets wounded in the back by shrapnel from a US mortar round in so doing. The "friendly fire" wound still earns Alex his second Purple Heart medal—and with it comes a promotion from corporal to buck sergeant—

but it is a hollow recognition in many ways as Alex grieves intensely for his lost brother who has been part of his life "forever." He misses old "Billy Bilgewater" almost as much, for they were comrades in arms ever since landing on Guadalcanal 1942. Alex and many other casualties are sent to Brisbane Australia on a hospital ship for—in Alex's case—a month of rest and recuperation, while the battle for Peleliu rages on and on.

The 7th Marines are assigned to take the southern part of Peleliu, known as "The Point." That takes nine days, after which Chesty Puller's 1st Marines and the surviving 7th assault a foreboding central ridge called the Umurbrogol which is honeycombed with caves and tunnels. Casualties continue mounting. When the shattered 7th finally gets pulled out of the line, the 5th Marines are transferred from their static guard duty at the captured airfield—that is already in use by Marine Corsairs to help the infantry with air-to-ground support—and are moved over to replace the 7th. The Army's 321st Regimental Combat Team (RCT) is also brought ashore to assist the 1st and 5th Marines, and a week later on October 30th the full Wildcat Division takes over the Peleliu campaign to relieve the Old Breed and finish the cleanup of the island.

On November 27th the island is finally declared secure, nearly a month after the rescheduled Philippine campaign has already started, thereby confirming that Peleliu was not really needed! The Umurbrogol becomes known as "Bloody Nose Ridge." Casualties are unusually high for the Americans on Peleliu, with 1,544 killed and 6,843 wounded. Nearly all 11,000 Japanese are killed, and just a few hundred prisoners are taken.

*US Marines on Peleliu with M4 Sherman Tanks*

A Japanese lieutenant and 32 men somehow manage to hold out in the ghastly Umurbrogol caves until April 1947, nearly two years after Japan officially surrenders, when they are finally persuaded to surrender as well! Such was the fierce dedication and determination of many Japanese warriors in the Pacific War. Japan was indeed a formidable adversary.

## *** LIFE GOES ON ***

After the Old Breed gets relieved by the Army's 81st on Peleliu, those of the battered Marines who were still standing are taken back to Pavuvu to reclaim their sanity and mobility.

When Alex Jones and others get released from hospital in Brisbane, Alex persuades the head doctor to grant him two weeks' leave, which he uses for visiting Ajax's young widow Mary Ellen and her infant son Able in Melbourne, to deliver the sad news about Ajax.

Mary Ellen is deeply shocked to learn about Ajax's death, and they have a good cry together. During the next few days, as she reacquaints Alex with the sights of Melbourne and he dines several times with her and her parents, their mutual sorrow gradually turns to mutual admiration and then into mutual affection.

"Alex, how is it that your parents named you twins with such similar names?"

"Well, Mary Ellen, I would like to say it's a long story, but it really isn't," Alex replies. "My folks picked out my name well in advance before they knew my mom was carrying twins. In fact they didn't know about the twins until Ajax popped out after I did. Well, my granddad's name is Alexander Jones but they thought that name was too long, so I was to be called Alex, period."

"That makes sense. We Aussies like short names too, but what about Ajax? Who was he named after?"

"No one in our family, but in Norman Oklahoma where we lived there is a big university and the professor of ancient languages is—or was, he passed away last year—Mom's cousin. When my dad went to see him after we twins were born, asking for a name for my brother, the professor came up with Ajax, which is supposedly the name of an ancient Greek hero. There wasn't time to ask other friends for suggestions because the hospital required names for both of us babies before they would let the family go home, which would have cost my parents another day's expenses. So, Ajax it was. But how did you and Ajax pick Able for the baby's name?" he counters, grinning.

"Ha! Well, Ajax wanted another name that started with 'A,' so your good old Marine Corps provided the answer. When I wrote him that I was pregnant—I guess he was at some place called Pavuvu—he wrote back that the Corps insists that A is called Able—you know, Able, Baker, Charlie, Dog, etc." *(if that happened nowadays, the list would be Alpha, Bravo, Charlie, Delta, etc – Ed.}*

Alex cracks up at that story. "Hey, that's really funny. He never told me you were expecting, and I guess he was too embarrassed to say his child would be named by our phonetic alphabet. Good thing it wasn't a girl, eh?"

Before the two weeks were up, Alex and Mary Ellen agree to be married after he is released from the Marine Corps, and also agree that he will officially adopt little Able as his son, which is required under Australian law if the youngster is to have any civil rights in future years. Alex and Mary Ellen's commitment is the beginning of their mutual love, and is also a private memorial to Ajax, who will remain beloved by both.

"Mary Ellen, when will your brother be back home?" Alex asks. "I was hoping to meet him and get acquainted."

"Well, he was home for a while after Rommel was defeated in North Africa," she replies, "but his Aussie 9th Division is still in New Guinea until General MacArthur releases it. Don't worry, you two will meet at our wedding!"

As he prepares to return to Brisbane for a medical checkup and onward transportation to Pavuvu, Alex tells Mary Ellen the reason the twins joined the Marines in the first place.

"Dear girl and wife-to-be, you need to know about something important. When Ajax and I were at Oklahoma University, we both fancied ourselves in love with the same girl, who was a student like us. She kept stringing both of us along and making us each feel like her beau, but we finally figured out that we were just her backup plan in case the apple of her eye didn't fancy her enough to get married. When that dawned on us, we dropped out of OU and followed OUR backup plan, which was to join the good old Crotch. Oops, sorry, I meant to say the Corps. Well I guess we were fated to fall in love with the same girl once again."

"Oh Alex, that's so beautiful. I'm glad that you both got to Oz so that I could be that fated girl for each of you. And I'm so thrilled that you agree to come back here to live and work for Daddy, just like Ajax would have done. But we must go to Oklahoma on our honeymoon to see your parents."

## *** THE BATTLE OF LEYTE GULF ***

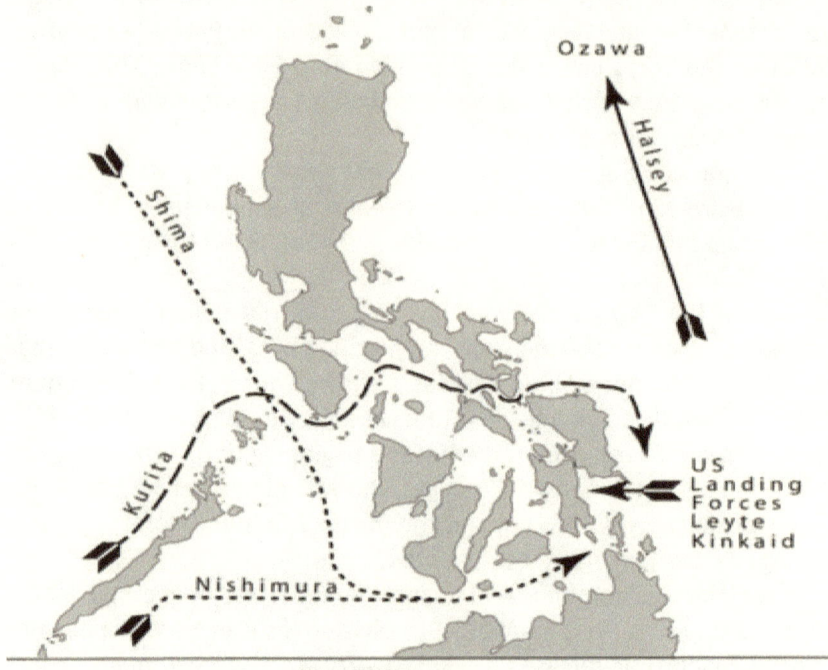

### The Philippines
The Japanese plan to repel the American invasion at Leyte--Oct. 1944.

Japan had anticipated for some time an Allied attack to recover the Philippines, doubtless from hearing through its spy network that General MacArthur had sworn over and over to return there in force. When the Allies began their new campaign on Leyte instead of Mindanao, the Japanese designed a clever but complex plan for the IJN to defeat the US Navy and prevent any landings from taking place.

The preceding map outlines the Japanese plan, which was first of all to lure Halsey's 3rd Fleet and its fast aircraft carriers away from Leyte. This was accomplished by Admiral Ozawa making a feigned attack from the north with the Japanese carriers which, because of recent attrition in the Marianas, had very few actual aircraft on board. After Halsey's planes battle successfully with Japanese land-based planes from Luzon and also help sink Kurita's super battleship *Musashi* (a sister ship of *Yamato* with 18-inch guns), Halsey takes the decoy bait and chases north after the southbound Japanese carriers, which promptly reverse direction as if cowed by Halsey's quick reaction, thus luring Halsey even further away from Leyte Gulf.

Unfortunately—perhaps assuming that Kurita's Central Force is in retreat after losing the *Musashi*—Halsey takes all six of his fast battleships on the northward chase in addition to the carriers, and thereby leaves the San Bernardino Strait to the north of Samar and Leyte unguarded and open to the rest of Admiral Kurita's still powerful fleet, with its intent to destroy MacArthur's landing forces.

This decision by Halsey leaves the landing force protected only by Admiral Kinkaid's 7th Fleet battleships and cruisers, which are south of Leyte together with some light carriers. When Kurita's Central Force does in fact burst forth unopposed from the San Bernardino Strait to threaten the Allied landings, his ships are so aggressively attacked by an ad hoc collection of 450 aircraft from Kinkaid's sixteen light carriers that Kurita assumes he is being attacked by planes from Halsey's fleet carriers once again. In consequence, he promptly withdraws his fleet to safety, including the *Yamato*, and the Allied landing force is not attacked by Kurita. (*This splendid action by the light carriers is the subject of Jim Hornfischer's great book* The Last Stand of the Tin Can Sailors, *which is listed in the bibliography – Ed.*)

Meanwhile the as-yet combined Southern Force of Admirals Nishimura and Shima—some forty miles apart with Nishimura in the lead and unsure of Shima's whereabouts—proceeds toward the Surigao Strait south of Leyte. Nishimura's force is at first intercepted by flotillas of US destroyers and PT Boats that sink and damage some of his cruisers and destroyers, and also alert Admiral Kinkaid's main force in Leyte Gulf.

Thanks to this early warning, the Nishimura residue—upon emerging into Leyte Gulf—is promptly set upon by Kinkaid's six old prewar battleships (five of which were repaired after the Pearl Harbor attack), that succeed in sinking one of Nishimura's battleships and several cruisers. At that point, Nishimura withdraws his even smaller residue away from Leyte Gulf, only to encounter Shima's trailing force heading in his direction. This encounter creates much confusion and some collisions.

It is clear, after the battle ends, that both sides were hampered to a critical degree by the lack of unified command structures. Halsey reported to Nimitz whereas Kinkaid reported to MacArthur, thus neither was fully aware of what the other was planning and doing as there was no single leader in charge of the US ships.

In the Japanese case, all three fleets were subjected to strict radio silence by the war chiefs in Tokyo, therefore Nishimura and Shima were unaware of each other's location and were prevented from unifying their forces. Likewise Kurita, from not knowing where the other Japanese ships were located, lost the opportunity to coordinate with them and destroy the Allied landing forces.

The Battle of Leyte Gulf, which was effectively the end of the Japanese navy as a fighting force *(except for super battleship* Yamato *which will get its comeuppance in the battle for Okinawa – Ed.)*, is considered to be the largest naval conflict in history, with over 200,000 naval personnel participating. It is also the second and last time that battleships fight one another in WWII, the first occasion being earlier in the Solomons, as the reader may recall.

## *** RECOVERING THE PHILIPPINES ***

Invading the Philippines was a tricky business for the Japanese in 1942, just as it must have been for the Spanish three centuries before. The reason was that the many large and small islands, whose guardians needed to be subdued, always presented a literally awesome challenge for an invader. An invasion of the Philippines was never to be casually attempted without ample resources in materiel, manpower, and money.

Contrary to his vocal "I Shall Return" pledge and flamboyant public persona, General Douglas MacArthur was well aware of the formidable challenge that awaited him and the United States. He carefully studied what the Japanese had accomplished when they breached his old-fashioned defenses after the Pacific War began.

Conquering the Philippines was a tough job when the US prevailed in the Spanish-American War of 1898 too. In 1945 the US would be challenged there once again. *Déjà vu!*

## *** LEYTE, MINDORO, AND LUZON ***

Thankfully spared from the intricate naval strategy that the Japanese tried to implement for destroying the US invasion force off Leyte, the US Sixth Army came ashore there on 20 October 1944, using Filipino guerillas to organize the civilian population and keep roads clear so Leyte could be promptly freed of Japanese control. The preceding famous photo of Gen. MacArthur wading ashore on Leyte with President Sergio Osmeña (far left with pith helmet) was widely circulated to promulgate the general's "I have returned" message.

After securing Leyte—although renegade Japanese groups continued fighting there until the war ended in August 1945—American troops next occupied the island of Mindoro, just south of Luzon. This intermediate step was to provide airstrips so long-range P-51B Mustang fighter planes could give air support to the main objective, the island of Luzon and the capital Manila. Mindoro was only lightly garrisoned by the IJA and was fairly quickly controlled with the help, once again, of Filipino guerillas. The American fleet off Mindoro was heavily attacked by Japanese Kamikaze suicide planes, however, which antiaircraft fire from the ships had to deal with until new airfields were ready for use.

Luzon itself was a different story; it was very heavily defended. A vast number of US troops came ashore at Lingayen Gulf on the west coast of Luzon; over 170,000 of them. General Walter Krueger's Sixth Army had ten US divisions and five independent regiments under his command, more than the US sent ashore for any of the European landings, including Normandy. MacArthur was taking no chances! Later on, the US Eighth Army was added, mainly to clear out the southern Philippine islands.

As Americans fought their way onto Luzon, the Japanese fell back to Bataan and Corregidor Island in Manila Bay, just as the Americans had done in 1942 when the Japanese first arrived. But where things got bogged down was in the recapture of Manila, the capital city known as "The Pearl of the Orient."

Even though the IJA had surrendered on Luzon, the Japanese navy still had charge of Manila. Entrenched within the three-foot-thick walls of the old Spanish inner city under control by a detachment of Japanese Marines (SNLF - Special Naval Landing Force), the admiral in charge refused to surrender the city in spite of being repeatedly ordered by Lt. General Yamashita Tomoyuki (山下 奉文)to do so.

General Yamashita—known as "the Tiger of Malaya" for his cleverly planned and executed conquest of Malaya and Singapore—was given the last-minute responsibility for the Philippine defense after General Homma was removed on Tokyo's orders.

Frustrated once before by trying to stop the excess atrocities of the *Kempeitai* secret police in Singapore, the general was once again frustrated by Rear Admiral Iwabuchi's repeated refusal to obey his order to surrender Manila. The US Army was forced to destroy much of Manila and its "city within the walls" in order to eradicate the Japanese naval stubbornness. Nearly 100,000 Filipino civilians died in the month-long crossfire and from deliberate killings by the Japanese defenders.

*The brutal destruction of Manila*

Controversially, Yamashita was hanged in 1946 after a postwar trial, in essence for allowing the destruction of Manila to be brought about by the IJN's refusal to capitulate, and for atrocities committed by renegade members of the naval forces that were theoretically placed under his command. In spite of appeals to Admiral Nimitz and to President Truman, the execution took place.

Reoccupation of the Philippines was essentially a MacArthur show, although Australian—and even Mexican—air squadrons lent support to the US Army and to the USAAF.

Carlos Garcia Ortiz and Bernie Cruz are two young Mexican pilots who were trained at Randolph Field in San Antonio, Texas. They are Mexican citizens and school friends from Xalapa in the state of Veracruz. After their more advanced training ends, they and their squadron 201 are transferred to New Guinea by ship and then onwards to Manila Bay in the

Philippines in a convoy along with other fliers and some American troops. On their first morning at Clark Field, the entire Mexican squadron gets formed up when several cars drive into the base and park near the hangar as the squadron is called to attention.

*"Mira Bernie,"* says Carlos after the squadron is formed up, *"Allá está el famoso General MacArturo con su señora. Parece que nos van a dar la bienvenida."*

*"O viceversa, hermano,"* replies his companion, *"y aquel señor al lado de MacArturo que tiene una bandera en la mano, quizás es el presidente de este país o alguien importante por lo menos. ¿Qué piensas?"*

*"Bueno, es posible, pero el sombrero que tiene es un poco raro ¿no es cierto?"*

Carlos and Bernie are suddenly interrupted by the screech of a microphone as a portable sound system is quickly set up by some airmen and a civilian. The young pilots are correct; the man with the pith helmet is indeed the Philippine president. After a few words of gratitude to the Mexican squadron's colonel and his formation of pilots and ground crew, President Sergio Osmeña, who speaks in both English and Spanish, introduces General Douglas and Mrs. Jean MacArthur to the formation. The general speaks afterwards:

"My dear friends from Mexico. I have been honored to know your wonderful country for many years, going back to when I was a young student at the Texas Military Institute in San Antonio Texas, just as you were recently in that great city for your training. Unfortunately I can no longer speak your beautiful language, so I hope President Osmeña will be kind enough to translate these words on my behalf."

The president nods, rustling the script that is in his other hand, as the general continues:

"It is my great honor today to present your squadron 201 with this Mexican battle flag," (which the president passes over to him), "and to ask your squadron leader to please come forward and receive it."

The speech goes on for some ten minutes and is duly translated by President Osmeña, at which point the Mexican colonel marches smartly forward and bows to Mrs. MacArthur, then salutes the general and the president. After receiving the battle flag, the squadron leader does an about face and lifts the flagstaff high.

*"¡Viva México! ¡Un aplauso, caballeros, por favor!"* At that point the formation breaks into a frenzy of cheers and applause.

Squadron 201, flying the latest P-47 Thunderbolt fighter planes, goes on to glory with air-to-ground support for the US Sixth Army that is still trying to corner Japanese fighters in the northern Luzon hills and jungles.

When the Japanese Army in the Philippines under General Yamashita finally surrenders, Squadron 201 becomes part of a long range bombing campaign to neutralize Formosa, flying their P47s with a heavy bomb below the starboard wing and an extra fuel tank under the port wing. It is quite challenging to maintain the plane's equilibrium as the fuel tank is gradually drained, and then again when the bomb is abruptly dropped.

## ** OKINAWA, FORMOSA, KOREA, MANCHURIA **

Okinawa and Formosa are substantial islands that were under Japanese control from 1879 and 1895 respectively, and were considered to be part of Japan itself. Korea, a mainland peninsula, was a Japanese colony from 1910, as was Manchuria from 1931, also located on the mainland. The Allies, after the defeat of Japan, decided to handle each of those four Japanese territories in different ways, but in the meantime they all needed to be captured or isolated.

Okinawa, the smallest of the four at slightly less than 900 square miles, was defended by 100,000 Japanese veterans and 55,000 irregular troops. There were also several hundred thousand civilian villagers on the island. Just 350 miles from Japan, Okinawa was duly scheduled for invasion. Its Operation Iceberg was in fact the largest US amphibious invasion of the entire Pacific War.

Beginning on 1 April 1945, the multiservice US Tenth Army—consisting of the First and Sixth Marine Divisions with the Second Marine Division in reserve, and the Army's 7th and 96th Infantry Divisions—went ashore on Okinawa, meeting only token resistance at first. Operation Iceberg was placed under the command of the US Army's Lt. General Simon Bolivar Buckner Jr., whose previous WWII job was the defense of Alaska and the recapture of the Aleutian Islands, with mediocre results. Buckner fancied himself a hard charger, and lived up to that image by running his troops head on into Japanese defences, a prewar tactic that unfortunately brought about a high level of US casualties.

Soon after the Okinawa campaign began, Japan—in an act of desperation—sent the super-battleship *Yamato* to Okinawa to be beached and used for bombarding US forces with its huge 18-inch guns. *Yamato* was given just enough scarce fuel to make a one-way trip. However, the great ship was spotted en route by US submarines, and 5th Fleet carrier planes were quickly called over to attack. On April 7th, writhing alone without air cover in an effort to dodge torpedoes, in a one-sided battle against an armada of US aircraft, *Yamato* was sent to the bottom, taking her admiral and captain and some 3,000 crew members to a watery grave.

It was a grim reminder of Japan's having dispatched British battleship HMS *Prince of Wales* three years earlier off Malaya.

*IJN Yamato and an escort under attack en route to Okinawa*

*(An intended sister ship to Yamato and Musashi, IJN Shinano was sunk by an American submarine off the coast of Japan while undergoing sea trials. On the orders of Admiral Yamamoto, Shinano's half-completed hull was converted from a super-battleship into an aircraft carrier, the largest in the world – Ed.)*

After the Okinawa landings commenced, Marines were assigned the northern part of the island, with the Army in charge of the south. It turned out that the north was only lightly defended because Japanese planners established their main defensive positions in the form of a concentric ring of obstacles among the more rugged and hilly southern interior. That concentrated defense was very effective, causing the Army a high number of casualties with little penetration. Even with Marine units being brought south to augment the Army divisions, the battle for Okinawa was long and arduous.

## *** CHANGING OF THE GUARD ***

On April 12th, 1945, during his fourth successive term, an ailing President Franklin Delanor Roosevelt passes away, and is succeeded by Vice President Harry S. Truman. The nation mourns FDR's passing, particularly since the wartime leader was unable to bring the massive conflict of World War Two to a successful conclusion and an Allied triumph.

On May 8th, 1945, when the war ends in Europe and VE Day is celebrated by huge crowds in New York's Times Square and elsewhere around the world, that momentous event is hardly even noticed on Okinawa where US Troops are still struggling to dislodge Japanese defenders from their formidable defenses. Near the end of the campaign, when the Japanese seemed to be losing their customary resilience, General Buckner—who often visited the front lines in a jeep with his three-star flag attached and waving for all to see—is killed by shrapnel from an incoming round that was clearly intended for him. He is replaced temporarily by Major General Roy Geiger USMC, the multi-talented Marine aviator who previously oversaw several Marine landings in the Pacific.

Geiger is promoted to lieutenant general on the spot and becomes the only Marine to ever command a full-size multi-division US Army. On his watch, Okinawa hostilities are finally ended and he declares the island secure on June 22nd, 1945. Japanese Lt. General Ushijima Mitsuru, who conceived and led the strong defense against overwhelming Allied strength, commits ritual suicide.

Not long afterwards, the Army brings over Lt. General "Vinegar Joe" Stillwell from his liaison role with Chinese Generalissimo Chiang Kai-Shek, to replace General Geiger and to prepare for leading the Tenth Army in the planned upcoming invasion of the Japanese homeland. A fine commander, Stillwell was sidelined in China due to a self-inflicted "wound"—his in-depth knowledge of China and its languages!

*Ruins of Naha, the capital of Okinawa*

Kamikaze attacks on the Allied fleet off Okinawa are intense throughout the campaign, in spite of equally intense anti-aircraft gunnery. The Allied fleet loses over 30 small ships, while many larger ones get seriously damaged. It was difficult to comprehend how young Japanese pilots could consent to undergo training for months and then wing their way from Kyushu to dive their planes into oblivion in the name of their emperor. Japan was certainly a formidable adversary!

After Okinawa is secured and a provisional military government is set up, American and Mexican fighter squadrons move there from the Philippines to free up the American carriers that are constantly being targeted by Kamikazes. These Allied land-based planes also intensify their raids on Formosa to the south and occasionally on the Japanese island of Kyushu to the north, where an Allied invasion is planned to take place later in late 1945.

In addition to the larger island of Formosa, the mainland Japanese colonies of Manchuria and Korea are also bombed by the Allies in order to observe the Japanese responses and to keep Japan guessing as to where and when the next inevitable invasion will commence.

Formosa, as Taiwan was known to the Allies in those days, is considered too large for a preliminary invasion, as is Manchuria—which the Japanese renamed Manchukuo after they took it away from China in 1931. As for Korea, alternatively known as "The Hermit Kingdon," the Allies considered it too remote from Japan proper to be of any strategic use.

Nevertheless it is agreed that all four of those former Japanese possessions will definitely be occupied and "decontaminated' after the war ends. The only question is, which of the Allies can do the occupying? The likely candidates are the United States, China, and Russia, the latter ally having helped the US and Britain defeat Germany. Russia's leader Josef Stalin promised FDR to join the Asia-Pacific war effort by August, which the Russians are doing with vigor by liberating Manchuria.

What is unknown, even to top US commanders in the Pacific theater—who are marshalling their resources in preparation for a massive invasion of Japan that is expected to last for well over a year and result in a million or more casualties—is that the US has tested a deadly new weapon that might conceivably forego the need for such an invasion. The secret weapon will later become known as the Atomic Bomb, and its components were being secretly transferred to the Marianas for deployment in Japan by B-29 bombers.

## *** ANOTHER TERRIBLE TRAGEDY ***

A late-war tragedy for the US Navy is the sinking of heavy cruiser USS Indianapolis (CV-35) by Japanese submarine I-58 on 30 July 1945. The veteran ship often served as the Fifth Fleet flagship under Admiral Spruance. She more recently underwent repairs at Mare Island in California after bomb damage off Okinawa, and then sailed from San Francisco to Pearl Harbor followed by a high-speed run to Tinian in the Marianas to deliver critical components for the first atomic bomb. Afterwards she was sailing unescorted from Guam to the Philippines to rejoin the US fleet when two torpedoes struck and she went down in twelve minutes, but was able to broadcast an SOS. Three US shore stations received the SOS but none acted on it! When the ship failed to reach Leyte on its ETA of 31 July, no report was made that she was overdue.

*USS Indianapolis after refit at Mare Island*

Of the 1196 men aboard, around 300 were lost with the ship. Nearly 900 more were afloat in life jackets and a few rafts with scant food and water, suffering from the elements and savage shark attacks for nearly four days before their greatly reduced numbers were finally spotted by two routine patrol planes that dropped life rafts and immediately summoned help. There were ultimately just 316 survivors, making 880 the largest loss of life from a single ship in US naval history.

## *** THE ONI INVESTIGATES ***

When news of the *Indianapolis* sinking and delayed recovery reaches Naval Headquarters on Guam, Rear Admiral Stanley "Stoney" Wall of the ONI becomes quite incensed. He lets loose at one of Admiral Nimitz's aides.

"What the hell is so screwed up with our ship tracking procedures that a major warship can disappear for nearly four days after getting torpedoed, without anyone even wondering why it is overdue? Damn, if the patrol planes hadn't happened to see those poor bastards floating in the ocean, we might have lost the entire crew without ever knowing what happened! As it is, more people were lost after the sinking than went down with the ship!"

After learning that some of the survivors were transported to a US field hospital on Peleliu in the Palau Islands and others were taken to a similar facility on Samar in the Philippines, the admiral promptly sends orders to Commander Perkins in Sydney and Lt. McGowan in Leyte, to go and interview each of the survivors to get their stories and find out what had happened, and whether the ship sent any message before it went down.

In due course, Bongo reports from Peleliu that the ship's captain and the duty radio operator both survived the sinking and the ordeal afloat. There had indeed been an SOS transmitted, and duly acknowledged by at least one recipient.

"Most of the men are recovering from severe dehydration, sir," Bongo reports. "The skipper told me there were many deaths from shark attacks and from drinking salt water, and even from suicide. It was a tough ordeal. Would you like me to come over to Guam to testify?"

"No, Bongo, but thanks for visiting those poor fellows. McGowan reported more or less the same thing from Samar, as he was practically next door on Leyte. There's bound to be an official inquiry, though, in which case you and McGowan may be needed as eyewitnesses to the survivors' condition and their comments. We'll get back to you on that. Meanwhile try to find out who received the SOS, will you—and why there were no reports about that either."

"Aye, aye sir," Bongo replies, thinking how sad President Roosevelt would be, had he lived to get the news of having lost another of his favorite heavy cruisers, just like the USS *Houston* that was sunk back in '42 off Java.

Bongo is also glad that the ONI is no longer responsible for the PT-Boat squadrons, which had been the case before the Pearl Habor attack. That in turn reminds him of Admiral Brady who managed to retire from the Navy in 1942. *Lucky fellow: he's probably putting about in his vegetable garden nowadays,* Bongo imagines.

There is indeed an *Indianapolis* inquiry after the war—and a court martial. The Navy attempts to place the blame for the ship's loss on its captain, who survived the sinking, but eventually he is fully exonerated with help from the Japanese captain of the submarine I-58, who also survived the war.

*(The ship's wreck was discovered in 2017 by Paul Allen's deep diving research vessel Petrel, in 18,000 feet of water – Ed.)*

# CHAPTER EIGHT

## *** *JAPAN SURRENDERS* ***

On 6 August 1945, a B-29 (named *Enola* Gay after the pilot's mother) takes off from Tinian in the Marianas to drop a uranium-based atomic bomb nicknamed "Little Boy" on Hiroshima Japan. The effect is catastrophic, killing thousands of mostly civilian people instantaneously and many more thousands later on from the after-effects of burns and radiation. The city of Hiroshima is flattened, but Japan's military still refuses to surrender and Emperor Hirohito still refuses to distance himself from that decision, even though a prince of his royal family had suggested abdication to the emperor in February 1945.

*The Hiroshima explosion*

The US had only two more atomic bombs available in the Marianas. Rather than conserve them, a decision is taken to use another one quickly so that Japan might assume the Americans have a limitless supply. Consequently *Bockscar*, also a Tinian-based B-29, takes off on 9 August with a plutonium-based bomb nicknamed "Fat Man." Nagasaki, its secondary target, is selected for the raid because the primary target city of Kokura was obscured by clouds that day. The result in Nagasaki is similar to the Hiroshima devastation. Fat Man is significantly more powerful than Little Boy, but parts of Nagasaki were sheltered by hills from the blast and the actual destruction is slightly less than Little Boy's ruination, but still horrendous.

*The more powerful Nagasaki explosion*

Also on 9 August, Russia—partially recuperated from the Battle of Stalingrad with Germany—declares war on Japan, as Stalin had promised

Roosevelt. Soon afterwards, the Russians commence an invasion of Man-chukuo, the former territory of Manchuria that Japan seized from China in 1931.

The American super-bombs and the Russian invasion cause heated debate among the leadership in Tokyo. Although some ultra-militants want to continues the war, and even attempt a coup during the night of 14 August, the Emperor announces on 15 August 1945 that Japan will surrender unconditionally as the Allies insist, with Japan's only request being the preservation of its monarchy. To this the Allies agree—in spite of some public anger toward Emperor Hirohito—feeling that Japan's monarchy will be needed for effective postwar stability and reconstruction.

*General MacArthur accepts the Japanese surrender*

The formal Japanese surrender is signed on board battleship USS *Missouri* in Tokyo Bay on 2 September 1945, with General MacArthur and a host of Allied senior officers observing the long sought-after event. Standing at attention behind MacArthur when he signs for the Allies, are the emaciated former POWs, British Lt. General Percival who in 1942 surrendered Singapore and Malaya, and US Lt. General Wainwright who  surrendered Corregidor and the Philippines the same year. They had both been interned in Manchukuo. If the surrender was an emotional moment for them, they didn't display it, but when VJ Day got announced in the Allied countries on 15 August 1945, the public response was certainly emotional.

Millions of servicemen and women who might otherwise have been killed or wounded during the planned invasion of Kyushu Japan, suddenly had a new lease on life. This iconic VJ Day photo taken by Alfred Eisenstaedt of a sailor kissing a nurse in New York City was published in Life Magazine.

For US Servicemen who were still in the Pacific, VJ Day was important, but sometimes just casually organized.

*Lt. Cdr. W. A. Clark Jr USNR (with shirt and cap) and staff members on Okinawa*

## *\*\*\* OCCUPATION AND WAR TRIALS \*\*\**

As soon as the Japanese surrender is announced, the Third Amphibious Corps (IIIAC) consisting of the First and Sixth Marine Divisions is sent to North China to disarm and repatriate Japanese troops which—together with Japanese civilians in China—number over six hundred thousand persons! IIIAC, the "New China Marines," soon find themselves in the middle of a civil war between the Chinese Nationalist Army (CNA) and the Chinese Communists. IIIAC remains on site until 1949, when Chinese Communists prevail over the CNA whose residue flee to Taiwan *(taking with them many treasures from the Palace Museum in Beijing; some of which are on view today in the National Palace Museum of Taipei – Ed.).*

Trying their best to remain neutral as the civil war rages on, but being tasked with helping the Nationalist Chinese government with its Japanese repatriation chore, Marines are often fired upon by Communist cadres while guarding trains and bridges. Frequently too, rather than joining the masses of their countrymen being repatriated to Japan, many Japanese soldiers decide to join one or the other Chinese army as mercenaries where their disciplined skills are highly valued, but eventually those Japanese get repatriated as well.

By the summer of 1946, the repatriations are completed and IIIAC's role reverts to protecting American property and civilians, as its strength is gradually drawn down from 57,000 to around 25,000. In 1949, the last Marines are withdrawn from China.

In Japan itself, it is the task of the US Sixth and Eighth Armies to bring about reconstruction and to reorganize the civil government. This effort is led by General MacArthur as Supreme Commander for the Allied Powers. The first task was to feed the starving populace; hence MacArthur issues an immediate edict that Allied personnel are forbidden to buy any food or drink from local shops until further notice. For the rest of 1945, food is provided by US government agencies, and private donor agencies join the effort in 1946. With over 5 million Japanese citizens being repatriated from around the Pacific region, the task of feeding the nation remains a huge challenge for several more years.

Military disarmament was the next priority. By December 1945, all

Japanese military organizations are completely disbanded and unused weapons and ordinance are collected and dumped into the sea.

A new constitution is adopted, giving women equal status and all people the right to vote for government officials. Many other democratic norms are introduced and most are happily accepted by the populace. The national Shinto religion is abolished due to its militant nature. The emperor's role is changed to that of a symbolic nature, with all future authority resting in an elected government. The initial occupation by some 470,000 Allied troops in Japan is gradually reduced between 1945 and 1952, when the occupation is brought to an end and a Japanese self-defense force is authorized. Afterwards, the US gradually changes its relationship with Japan (and Germany) from an occupying force to a treaty partner. Today, the US still maintains aroundt 40,000 troops on some 50 bases in Japan and Okinawa, under mutual defense treaties between Japan and the US Pacific Command. Both Japan and Germany have been staunch US allies since the Cold War.

## *** THE USO RETURNS ***

Betsy's first postwar tour in the spring of 1946 brings her back to the Philippines and then to Korea. She and her colleagues do variety shows instead of two-act Broadway shows, which means several individual acts and some trios and quartets among the dancers.

Luzon—where Betsy learns that the veteran PT Boats from Morotai and New Guinea have been stripped and burned at sea after the war—is undergoing what will be a long reconstruction, especially for Manila's Intramuros, the old Spanish city center that was so very badly damaged by US forces while eviting a stubborn Japanese admiral and his special naval landing force. However, the countryside outside Manila begins to look nice and green, and some Filipinos are beginning to recover from the terrible trauma that the war had inflicted on them.

"Korea was not nice at all," Betsy writes to her mother. "Japan treated the Korean people as slaves, and they appeared sullen to me, and almost lifeless. Most were forced to do hard labor in the fields in order to keep Japan supplied with food. Korean men were drafted into the Japanese Army and used as POW camp guards, where their hatred of the Japanese was often directed at the prisoners under their care."

Sadism by Korean camp guards becomes one of the most frequent complaints reported by starving Allied prisoners after liberation. Quite often, young Korean women and girls were transported to Japan or their occupied islands for prostitution, where they were known more politely as 'comfort women,' Some women became willing mistresses of high-ranking Japanese officers as a means to be fed and clothed properly. Who could blame them?

During her tour of Korea to entertain US garrison troops, Betsy and her friends sometimes walked about Seoul, the capital, accompanied by soldiers for their safety, in the hope of finding something of interest. Betsy was fascinated that local women would approach the blonds among her group to touch their heads, never before having seen hair of that color.

Betsy was quite relieved when her first postwar tour ended. The next one was on Japan itself, as the nation gradually recovered from

the devastation that the war had brought. US personnel were spread all over the Japanese islands during the occupation years 1945-52. The USO was called upon to provide entertainment and hospitality throughout. This time it was "showbiz" once again. Their new Broadway show was *Gingham Girl*, a quaint musical originally launched in 1922 and made into a 1927 movie. *(The troops must have been perplexed – Ed.).* On that tour, Betsy went all over Japan with the new troupe. In April 1947 she married Ralph English, the show's manager whom she knew back in prewar New York.

"Ralph, can we go visit a few places without the whole troupe?" Betsy asks when they are on their short honeymoon weekend in a Tokyo hotel on the Ginza. "I think we could both relax more that way."

"Why sure, sweetie. I was thinking the same thing too," Ralph replies. "How does this sound, for example: the Navy will be taking some top brass to the Bikini atoll for an overnight picnic soon, and as of now there are still a few seats up for grabs on the plane. Bikini is the place in the Marshall Islands where they exploded a small atomic bomb last year after evacuating all the locals. They say it's a beautiful place with a huge lagoon."

"Great, can you get someone to run the USO show without us? And when is the picnic?"

"It's not till mid-November, hon. They want people to stay away from the island for a while after the July bomb test, you know, just to be on the safe side."

"Safe from what, love?"

"Whatever they call it, the bomb's afterglow apparently. Nothing to worry about."

"It sounds great, Ralph, but heck that's over a month from now. I really need a break from this endless show routine as soon as we can. Isn't there somewhere we could go this coming week or next?"

"Um, well maybe. We're supposed to play for the garrison at Hiroshima next week, and Nagasaki a few days later. Maybe we can skip these if you really aren't up to it.

"Oh heck, I hate to be a spoil sport. Let's go ahead and hang in, then try to get away for a few more weekends after the Bikini thing, before we head for Europe, OK?"

## *** THE WAR CRIME TRIALS ***

The countless horrors of the Pacific war itself were augmented by many further instances of criminal behavior on the part of Japanese military and naval units and individuals against Allied combatants and civilians, plus countless Japanese barbarities against indigenous populations, primarily the Chinese.

After Japan surrendered in August 1945, a series of war crime trials were convened during subsequent years. The trials took place in both Japan itself and in the liberated territories that Japan had forcibly conquered and occupied. In each case, the accused individuals were provided with legal defense counsel, and witnesses were brought forth on behalf of both the prosecution and defense.

To prosecute high-level Japanese leadership, a Tokyo tribunal was established in April 1946. This tribunal could only prosecute Class A suspects, meaning those who could be charged with Crimes against Peace (causing the war) in addition to their other possible crimes. The tribunal tried 28 present and former prime ministers including Tojo Hideki and other high government and military officials, with Emperor Hirohito and members of the Imperial family being exempted by General MacArthur on the basis that removal of the emperor would cause wide resentment among the population and make the Japanese recovery more difficult. Seven of the defendants were sentenced to death and sixteen more to life imprisonment. The Tokyo tribunal was disbanded early in 1948, its work having been completed.

More than 5700 Class B and C suspects were tried at some 50 other tribunals in places like Manila, Singapore, Batavia, Guam, etc., where the alleged offenses took place, or else in Japan, China and Australia. Class B offenses were crimes against the laws and customs of war, and Class C offences were crimes against humanity. It is beyond the scope of this book to enumerate the many trials that took place between 1946 and 1951 or the grisly events that prompted them, but the following three examples may serve to illustrate the proceedings.

*Tojo's trial in Tokyo*

Example 1: The trial of Japan's wartime prime minister, General Tojo Hideaki. Tojo was seen by many in the US to embody the essence of Japanese militarism, expansionism, and cruelty. He, along with others, was tried in Tokyo as a Class A criminal for having caused the war in the first place. He attempted suicide after the Japanese surrender, but was resuscitated by American doctors. Tojo was found guilty and was sentenced to death by hanging, which was carried out in 1948.

Example 2: The trial of IJA General Yamashita Tomoyuki in Manila for Class B and C offenses. General Yamashita earned the sobriquet "Tiger of Malaya" for his astute and speedy conquest of Malaya and Singapore, capturing a British army four times the size of his own. During that conquest, several terrible atrocities were committed by soldiers under his command and by the *Kempeitai* secret police. When his soldiers eventually breached the causeway between Malaya and Singapore two

*General Yamashita, rear*

months later, Kempeitai brutality was particularly severe for any of Singapore's Chinese population that were perceived to have British contacts or anti-Japanese sentiments, some thirty thousand of whom were shot, bayonetted, or bound together in groups of three and dropped from launches into the harbor to drown. This was known in Singapore as the Sook Ching Massacre, which was eventually extended to Malaya and Penang.

General Yamashita was not tried for those atrocities, as it was felt that he was not personally responsible. However, he was tried and found guilty of the destruction of Manila and the massacre of thousands of Filipino civilians, both of which were caused by an IJN admiral not directly under Yamashita's command, and who repeatedly ignored his order to surrender. His defense counsel appealed the verdict to MacArthur, to the US Supreme Court, and to President Roosevelt. The latter two refused to hear the appeal, turning the decision back to MacArthur who upheld the verdict. The execution was carried out in 1946.

This particular trial set an international precedent that senior commanders could be held responsible for the actions of their subordinates, whether or not they had ordered those actions.

Example 3: The three trials of Major General Shoji Toshinari (Toshishige) for Class B and C offenses. As a colonel in the early days of the Pacific war, his 230th IJA "Shoji Regiment" (as it was sometimes known) stormed ashore 1 March 1942 on the north coast of West Java in the Dutch East Indies, aiming to capture an airport near Subang (Soebang in Dutch), which was the headquarters of P&T Lands, a large Anglo-Dutch plantation. Shoji's troops were opposed by some regular KNIL soldiers (Dutch infantry) and by members of the Java home guard that had been called to active duty when the war started. After a brief but fierce fight, Shoji's troops prevailed and began to take their revenge on the defenders and local civilians Wounded soldiers in the Subang hospital were bayonetted, and some surrendered KNIL soldiers, a young nurse from the hospital, and several Dutch plantation managers in the home guard were massacred and buried in a common grave.

For the atrocities committed by Shoji's troops against the 300 unarmed Dutch soldiers and civilians, Shoji was tried in Hong Kong after the war but the finding was "no case to answer." Later he was tried again in Singapore and found not guilty. Still later he was tried again in Batavia, the Dutch capital of Java. This time he was found guilty and sentenced to death in July 1949, but his sentence was later commuted to 8 years in prison. Shoji died in 1974 of natural causes.

Readers interested in further information about the Japanese atrocities and war trials in WWII can find a lot of detailed information on the Internet. Today it is still a controversial subject in both Japan and the United States. In Japan the war trials were considered to be acts of revenge, whereas in the US many people felt that too many other guilty perpetrators should have been hanged.

## *** FROM OCCUPATION TO ALLIANCE ***

As the Allied occupation of Japan wound down in the early 1950s, the relationship between Japan and the US was gradually transformed into a military alliance. Although a large number of US and Allied troops were withdrawn from Japan by 1951, many thousands remained *(and some are still there today – Ed.)*, ostensibly to help guard Japan from foreign enemies but also to keep an eye on internal developments. The pacifist constitution that that was thrust upon Japan early in the occupation was fervently embraced by the Japanese populace, to the extent that anti-war sentiment is still prevalent in the nation. Japan eventually allowed itself a Self-Defense Force—and Japan became a strong supporter of the US during the Cold War with Russia—but it is still political suicide in Japan to run for office on a full rearmament platform *(although there are militant sentiments among certain political factions in Japan today – Ed)*.

So, ironically or perhaps gratefully, the US finds itself committed to helping ensure the security of its one-time belligerent enemy by garrisoning troops and other military assets in Japan proper and in Okinawa. The emblem below from Marine Corps Air Station Iwakuni Japan is one such example.

*Moshi-moshi ano-ne, Iwakuni GCA*

Military Occupation eventually became Military Assistance in both Japan and its former colony of Formosa, later to be known as the Republic of China (ROC) on Taiwan. The Taiwan Military Assistance Advisory Group was formed in 1951, with oversight provided by the US Embassy in Taipei. The function of MAAG Taiwan was to help train the military forces of the ROC, which were under threat from the PRC (Peoples Republic of China, formerly known as Communist China under Mao Tse-tung) that had prevailed in China's civil war on the Chinese mainland in 1949. The ROC (formerly known as Nationalist China under Chiang Kai-shek) had been at war with Japan since 1937, then abruptly found itself involved in a civil war at home, which it lost.

With significant assistance from MAAG Taiwan, the former Japanese colony of Formosa eventually learned how to build its own fighter aircraft, the F5 being a splendid example. Later, a unique version of the F-16 was produced locally, using two F5 engines instead of the restricted-technology single engine developed for US-built F-16s.

MAAG Taiwan was dissolved in 1978 after the US derecognized the ROC and established formal ties with the PRC in Beijing. The world today still lives with the repercussion of that decision.

*MAAG Taipei office before bicycles yielded to motorcycles*

Japan had looked upon its Formosa colony as a valuable asset, and it invested heavily in the island's infrastructure and encouraged local investment in the development of manufacturing businesses, some of which are still operating today *(e.g. Formosa Plastics – Ed.)*.

Japan's treatment of its Korean colony was significantly harsher, although the Korean War that took place from 1950 to 1953—just a few years after the end of WWII—was more likely the result of the Allies having partitioned the former Japanese colony to allow the USSR to occupy its northern half. The rapid introduction of Communism to both China and North Korea became the spark that lit off the Korean war, which eventually led to the Cold War itself between the US and the USSR.

The status of the two Koreas is still unresolved today, the Korean war having been suspended by a Cease Fire rather than ended with an Armistice.

# EPILOGUE

Interracial and intercultural distain played a significant part in the outcome of World War Two and its aftermath. Had the Japanese been more welcoming to the local people in the islands that they had conquered, they might indeed have created a Pan-Asian universe—their much-touted Greater East Asia Co-prosperity Sphere—but instead the treatment of their hostages was terrible, not only the foreign colonial captives both civilian and military, but indigenous people as well, all of whom the Japanese considered to be inferior human beings.

It is an amazing transformation that Japan is nowadays a pacifistic nation that has foresworn its prior ambitions for conquering nearby nations. Japan became a rock-solid US ally in the Cold War and has remained steadfast in the face of aggression from the Peoples' Republic of China.

The main bone of contention between the US and Japan in the 21st Century is the ongoing occupation of Okinawa by several US military organizations, notably US Marines.

# END NOTES

## Postscript

PT-105 was among the first 80-foot Elco PT-Boats known as the "PT-103 Class," which were formed up in Panama for training and the defense of the Panama Canal in 1942, as Motor Torpedo Boat Squadron 5 (MTB RON-5), which consisted of twelve boats, PTs 103-114.

RON-5 was broken into two groups—PTs 103-108 and PTs 109-114—to be transported to the Pacific. The second group went first and was based at Tulagi and Rendova in the Solomon Islands. The second group went to the Russells and Rendova.

Lt. (jg.) USNR Richard Keresey (a.k.a. Gunga Din) was PT-105's first skipper, and later the author of a book named *PT-105*.

The photo below shows brand new PT-103 (foreground) and PT-105 (middle ground) packed up for delivery to Panama aboard a transport ship.

# Seguin Texas

*Old Seguin*

The origins of a small village on the Guadalupe River that would eventually become the City of Seguin (2022 POP 30,000) were not from the many German migrations to the Republic of Texas but instead from an earlier use by Texas Rangers as a watering stopover for chasing bandits farther west. In 1838 they named the place Walnut Springs, then in 1839 it was renamed Seguin to honor Juan Nepomuceno Seguin who had fought with the Anglos at the Alamo against a Mexican army, and who had accepted the Mexican surrender of San Antonio in 1836 on behalf of Gen. Sam Houston and the new Texas Republic.

Various German settlers did drop off later in Seguin, however, including a Jewish family named Seligmann from Bremerhaven in the 1860s and a Lutheran family named Saegert from Mecklenburg in 1883, both patriarchs of which had decided not to follow the main German migration corridor to New Braunfels and Fredericksburg, Texas, but instead to try their luck near Seguin which was rich in cotton-capable soil and later in oil production.

Descendants of these two Seguin families, who became classmate-friends from kindergarten through high school—probably because their surnames were in alphabetical order—were Clarence Saegert and

Elizabeth Seligmann. Elizabeth, better known as Betsy to her friends and family, was a strong-willed and precocious child who did not abandon those attributes as an adult. She decided in 1934 at the age of fifteen, with inspiration from several magazine articles, to go to New York and become a professional dancer. Her parents had divorced when she was five, so Betsy was able to convince her mother Blanche to accompany her as a chaperone. Betsy did attain her ambition and danced in several New York clubs, including Billy Rose's Diamond Horseshoe and various Broadway shows before joining the USO Camp Shows in 1944, which sent her Broadway troupe to the Pacific Theater.

Clarence, on the other hand, finished high school and initially attended TLC, the local Seguin college of higher learning (that later became TLU, a fully accredited Texas Lutheran University). Later he switched to the University of Texas in Austin, where he received a BS degree with honors. In 1942 he joined the Navy Reserve rather than risking the draft as the war effort expanded. The Navy made him an officer and assigned him to a PT Boat squadron in New Guinea as its XO (Executive Officer) in 1944. By 1945 he became one of the successive skippers of PT-105 in the Pacific Theater.

*Juan Seguin Monument in Seguin Texas*

## Fictional Characters

Blumberg, Olive and Valerie, mother and daughter friends of Blanche and Betsy Seligmann in Seguin.

Brady, RADM Ronald USN, head of ONI and PT Boats in Hawaii.

Bridgewater, Cpl. Billy USMC, ashore on Guadalcanal

Cruz, Bernie, a Mexican Air Force pilot attached to the USAAF

Fisher, Mabel, former GF of the Jones twins in Norman Oklahoma.

Garcia, Carlos Ortiz, another Mexican pilot with the USAAF

Jones twins Alex and Ajax, ex-OU Marines.

King, Valerie, stage name for Valerie Blumberg

McGowan, Ensign Robert USN and ONI

Perkins, Lt. Commander Elmer "Bongo" USN and ONI

Perry, Peter, British civil engineer

Thomas, Mary Ellen, Australian bride-to-be

Wall, Commodore Stanley "Stoney" USN and ONI

Silvers, Captain "Hi-Yo" USN, ONI liaison on CINCPAC staff.

## Abbreviations As Used In This Book

ASAP – As Soon As Possible/Practical

CO – Commanding Officer

HQ - Headquarters

ID – Identification (as in ID card)

MCRD – Marine Corps Recruit Depots in CA and NC

MTB – Motor Torpedo Boat, British and later US designation

NCO – Non-Commissioned Officer

OD – Officer of the Deck (Navy and Marines); of the Day (Army)

ONI – Office of Naval Intelligence

OSS – Office of Strategic Services, forerunner of the CIA

OU – The University of Oklahoma in Norman, OK

PT Boats – US Patrol Torpedo Boats, based on a British design

RAF – Royal Air Force (British)

RAAF – Royal Australian Air Force

TLC – Texas Lutheran College in Seguin, Texas (later TLU)

US – United States of America (sometimes just America for short)

USA – US Army

USAAF – US Army Air Force (later to become the US Air Force)

USCG – US Coast Guard

USMC – US Marine Corps

USN – US Navy

USO – United Services Organization

XO – Executive Officer

## Highly Recommended Further Reading

*Across the Reef,* Col. Joseph Alexander USMC (Ret.) 2013: The Marine Assault of Tarawa.

*At Close Quarters*, Robert L. Bulkley 1962 and 2017: PT Boats in the United States Navy, covering the Pacific and European Theaters.

*Bloody Beaches, The Marines at Peleliu*, BGen. Gordon Gayle USMC (ret.) 2013: A highly readable account of the controversial campaign.

*Embracing Defeat, Japan in the Wake of World War II*, John W. Dower 1999: Japan's occupation and transition into a US ally.

*Guadalcanal*, Richard B. Frank 1990: The definitive account of the landmark battle.

*Hostages to Fortune*, Arthur C. Nicholson III 2005: Loss of HMS *Prince of Wales and Repulse* off Singapore in December 1941.

*In Mortal Combat*, John Toland 1991: Korea 1950-1953

*MTBSTC: Motor Torpedo Boat Squadrons Training Center*, Charles C. Jones 2020: The PT Boat school at Melville RI.

*On the Warpath in the Pacific*, Clark G. Reynolds 2005: Admiral Jocko Clark and the Fast Carriers.

*South Pacific Cauldron*, Alan Rems 2014: World War II's great forgotten battlegrounds.

*Spotlight on Singapore*, Denis Russell-Roberts 1965: The fall of British Singapore.

*The Last Stand of the Tin Can Sailors*, James D. Hornfischer 2004: the US Navy's finest hour in the Battle of Leyte Gulf.

*The Marines in World War II*, Michael E. Haskew 2016: A Complete Encapsulation of the USMC under Fleet Admiral Chester Nimitz.

*They Were Expendable*, W.L. White 1942: PT Boats that helped Gen. MacArthur and family escape from the Philippines.

*PT-105*, Dick Keresey 2014: First skipper of this 80-foot ELCO boat: Actions in the Solomons.

*PT-109*, William Doyle 2016: War, survival and the destiny of John F. Kennedy.

## Poems for Betsy and Clarence (wherever they may be)

### OUR FRIEND BETSY
### And the USS PT-105

Our friend Betsy was a force of nature like sunshine, wind or rushing water, Her unfulfilled wish was for a family, with at least a son and daughter.

To New York City she went as a child to dance in Broadway shows, Times were hard, cash was dear, how she survived, not even she knows.

In wartime, Betsy danced her way across the South Pacific, Bringing joy to those whose lives in war were most horrific.

On stage one night she saw a friend ensconced in front row seating, After the show the two of them enjoyed a joyful meeting.

Clarence was skipper of a PT Boat, and lately from Seguin, He invited Betsy to take a ride in the bay she'd never seen.

Her answer was affirmative; "That's something I'd love to do!" So they all took a spin around the bay, including the rest of the crew.

The PT Boat got named *The Betsy*, and Betsy solemnly joined the crew,

Not only the skipper thought her special; from that short ride they all did too.

Carol Carpenter
18 June 2021

## OUR FRIEND BETSY RIDES AGAIN

Our friend Betsy was a wonder; no one else could steal her thunder. While still a girl she loved New York where her dancing gained some work. When Pearl Harbor made the news, New Yorkers hid and hit the booze. Eventually the USO took control of the New York show.

As World War Two consumed the world, Betsy joined a troupe that hurled Themselves across stormy oceans where weary troops (deprived of lotions) Came by hundreds from far and near to whistle and clap, to shout and cheer The skimpy costumed high-kicking dames that blinked their eyes and called them names.

One day Betsy's troupe did play on Morotai quite far away From New Guinea's swamps and camps where endless dancing gave them cramps. That day Betsy saw a friend from school perched upon a front-row stool. Clarence saw Betsy too and then, he gathered up his crew of men.

From PT-105 they came to meet the skipper's comely dame. Ere long they chose to take a ride with Betsy on the evening tide. The engines roared and off they went around the bay with no intent But the joy of being together with her. "Let's name our boat *Betsy*;" "Aye, aye sir!"

A solemn pledge was signed by all with a copy placed upon the wall Of the admiral's quarters on the shore, where tongue in cheek the admiral swore To keel-haul the lot of them, and have them flogged and flogged again. All this would happen if he could yet see any trace of a boat named *Betsy*.

Antwyn Price
19 June 2021

# About the Author

Singapore-born US Marine Corps veteran Antwyn Price was educated at Harvard College and the University of Oklahoma. His ongoing career as an engineer in California led to business opportunities in Latin America, the Far East, and Europe. In retirement, he and his wife Elizabeth made their home in the mountains of Mexico and the plains of Texas.

As an author, Antwyn's genre is historical fiction, which he likes to call 'faction' because his works are carefully built upon the factual historical record, "but adding some fictional characters makes for a more enjoyable read," he suggests.

Thus his books are human interest and adventure tales interwoven with the deeds of real historical personages.

This one, An Empire in Ruins, about the defeat of Japan in the Pacific region, is his final work of a trilogy about the Second World War in the Pacific Theater

https://www.antwynpricebooks.com

**◗ERN NAMES**

TAIWAN

PHILIPPINES

*balu*

*CELEBES
SEA*

○ *Sulawesi*

*Jaya Pura* ○

**PAPUA**
○ *Irian Jaya*

| 0 | | 500 Miles |
| 0 | | 500 KM |